THE CREATIVE

WRITER'S

COMPANION

THE CREATIVE WRITER'S COMPANION

SELLING YOUR IDEAS FOR
MOVIES, BOOKS, ELECTRONIC
MEDIA, AND MORE

STANLEY J. CORWIN

ST. MARTIN'S GRIFFIN 🙾 NEW YORK

Title page image used courtesy of Photodisc

www.stmartins.com

Book design by Victoria Kuskowski

Library of Congress Cataloging-in-Publication Data

Corwin, Stanley J.
    The creative writer's companion : selling your ideas
    for movies, books, electronic media, and more / Stan-
    ley J. Corwin.
        p. cm.
    ISBN 0-312-25276-5
    1. Authorship—Marketing.   I. Title.

PN161 .C67 2001
070.5'2—dc21

                                 00-045862

First Edition: April 2001

10 9 8 7 6 5 4 3 2 1

TO DAN GOLDSTEIN, MENTOR—WHO TAUGHT ME
A LOT.—FROM HIS MENTEE—WHO LISTENED.

CONTENTS

I am very grateful to the very special people in my life and career.

To my parents: my mom, Faye, and my late dad, Seymour, who taught me the love of words and books and ideas.

To my sister, Carole—the best friend any brother could ever wish for.

To my daughters, Donna and Ellen, and their growing families—Ron, Jonathan, Nathan, Rosalie, and Ray—who enrich my life, and many other lives.

To my daughter, Alexandra—a beautiful young lady who taught me to color outside the box.

To my wife, Donna—for her perks, her love, her inspiration—my own private muse.

To Al Secunda—a special friend, with love from the "Doctor."

To Ann Benya—who makes every manuscript better.

To Jane Dystel—an extraordinary agent, a dear friend. Thank you for the publishing journey we traveled together.

To Elizabeth Beier—a nurturing editor, an elegant lady.

To the gang at St. Martin's Press—thank you for making my creative ideas a publishing reality.

And to writers and creators everywhere—if I've helped you achieve your goals, I have enjoyed the process. *You* inspired me to write this book.

—STAN CORWIN

Believe it or not, we're in the middle of a revolution.

Only a few years ago, it seems, things were a lot simpler. A writer had an idea for a book or a screenplay, he or she sat down and wrote the particular play, novel, screenplay, romance, or whatever, and it ended at that. If the writer was fortunate enough to sell his or her work to a publisher, then the publisher was expected to market the book to the public. And once in a while, if the work became popular, then the rights to that book or play would be sold to Hollywood and turned into a major motion picture.

And that would be that.

Not anymore. The rules have changed, and today, the name of the game in creating a product is to invent something that can be marketed in several different areas, and thus "cross over" into different areas of the media. A movie is not just a movie anymore, nor is a book just a book, nor a TV show a TV show; instead, the initial product has become only a part of the total entity.

A movie or book in today's "vertical or horizontal" market, for example, can cross over and become an entire industry comprised of books, toys, games, sequels, worth several hundreds of millions of dollars.

Just take a look at *Star Wars, Where's Waldo?*, the various *Chicken Soup* books franchise, or *The Lion King*. Walk into a McDonald's or Burger King, and see what they offer their consumers: *Pocahontas* cups, *Toy Story* toys, special prizes you scrape off on their various cups, all of it related to the initial book, movie, or TV show.

In today's market, a book is not just a book; a book can be turned into a movie; a movie into a game; a movie into a game or into toy sold at one of the fast-food outlets around the country. At present, we're witnessing various *edutainment* concepts being transformed into DVDs and CD-ROMs. And with the amazingly rapid rise of the Internet and e-business and vertical platforms of business to business, we're literally standing on the edge of a marketing paradise.

How does this relate to you? How can you take your singular idea and convert it into a multimedia extravaganza?

If you want to know the answer to that, you've come to the right place, with the right book at the right time. Stan Corwin's excellent *The Creative Writer's Companion: Selling Your Ideas for Movies, Books, Electronic Media, and More* is exactly what we've all been looking for; a unique guide that steers us through the complex maze of marketing and merchandising areas of the current marketplace. Corwin's approach is so simple it's deceiving, yet it provides everything that will help you translate a single idea into a multimedia extravaganza.

What I found so inspiring reading this book is how much it expanded my awareness. Guided by Corwin's expertise, I'm learning to think with passion and enthusiasm about my own projects, not only as books or movies, but as CDs or DVDs, and about how they can be turned into various products. In other words, I'm beginning to understand what can or can't be done with my ideas.

The Creative Writer's Companion illuminates the opportunities of the multimedia market. Corwin's book takes the spark of an idea and brings it to a blazing fire of possibility. Stan Corwin shows you how your idea can be the pot of gold at the end of the rainbow.

—SYD FIELD
Beverly Hills, California

Syd Field is the world's bestselling author of screenplay books. *Screenplay, The Screenwriter's Workbook, Selling a Screenplay,* and *Four Screenplays* have sold several million copies, and have been translated into every major language. His books are used in over two hundred college film courses.

He is regarded as the "most sought-after screenwriting teacher in the world" (the *Hollywood Reporter*). Syd Field's screenwriting courses are featured on the Internet and on DVD, and his lectures and seminars are conducted throughout the world.

THE CREATIVE

WRITER'S

COMPANION

Once upon a recent time, an engaging artist from the English countryside by the name of Martin Handford drew an imaginative series of children's pictures in different settings. The intriguing concept of *Finding Waldo* was to locate this little elfish man in multicolored costume amid a myriad of objects and artifacts in a village, in a zoo, on a beach, etc. This cute and clever idea, with drawings deftly done in pen and ink, was a modest success in its British publication as a children's book.

Finding Waldo then became a craze, a media phenomenon that crossed the Atlantic. The original creative concept and idea of *Waldo*—the book—led to a myriad of books, games, puzzles, T-shirts, place mats, posters, calendars, and other mass merchandising products as well as a TV show. Everyone was soon asking *Where's Waldo?*, and the ensuing media blitz reflected the answer; he was everywhere.

A simple creative notion had succeeded far beyond the artist's imagination and become a licensing phenomenon. Its media exploitation was serendipitous, much like that of Barney and *Chicken*

Soup for the Soul and other merchandising manias of the past decade. Each new medium adapted the product of the previously successful medium and brought a new brand-name product to the marketplace. And each new format generated synergistic awareness and sales of the previous media entities. There were more *Waldo*s and *Harry Potter*s and *Chicken Soup*s to buy in various media configurations.

This kind of exploitation of a media product is often intended from the outset. The product is designed from the beginning to be packaged and merchandised as a myriad of licensed items.

When I was president of Tudor Communications in the late 1980s, author Gail Brewer Giorgio approached me with her written revelation that Elvis Presley did not die, complete with "evidence" that he was still alive. Gail appeared on *Larry King Live* and *Oprah* with her startling "facts" and generated a national public response.

We decided to rush the book *Is Elvis Alive?* into print. But there was a tape as well—a tape of Elvis speaking from somewhere "after his death." The tape was shocking and had to be heard. How could we combine our unusual media products—book and tape—into one commercial entity?

We created a cassette tape featuring two minutes

of the mysterious Elvis recording, and we simultaneously created a paperback book. The tape was affixed
to the front of the book with removable glue, and the
entire package was shrink-wrapped. The book sold the
tape; the tape sold the book—all in one $5.95 package.

This much-hyped, much-ballyhooed media product
was an instant rage. The book-and-tape elicited orders
for one-and-a-half million copies, extraordinary numbers for a trendy pop-cultural product. In fact, it was
so startlingly successful that it closed down our young
media company. The investors could not, would not
capitalize this media-exaggerated blowout. Neither
they nor we were prepared for Elvismania. The book—
with tape—became a *New York Times* bestseller. The
tape—with book—went to number one on the Walden
audio bestseller list. With some innovative marketing
we had tapped into Elvis fanaticism everywhere.

When Tudor, with Elvis book-and-tape, was eventually sold to a New York entity, I realized that this
fervent Elvis market had not been entirely satiated by
media products related to the legend who would never
die, literally or mythically. There was much more to
exploit. The lives and times of Elvis were not finished
just yet.

Gail and I formed a partnership and set out to create and produce an *Is Elvis Alive?* TV special. In a brief

period of time, *The Elvis Files* materialized. The two-hour nationally syndicated prime-time show, hosted by TV star Bill Bixby, aired live from the Imperial Palace hotel in Las Vegas.

Simultaneously we created a 900 number to call during the show (for $1.00) to register your opinion as to whether Elvis was still alive or dead. Incredible to imagine, over one million people made that call. Additionally, there was an 800 number to call to buy Elvis products, which included another book and a video—all not-so-coincidentally entitled *The Elvis Files*.

The total media blitz was a mega success. The TV special was seen on over two hundred stations by twenty million viewers and garnered a national rating of 9, which paralleled that of *Oprah* and *Jeopardy*. Everything "Elvis" sold in abundant numbers. Despite the many skeptics and cynics, Elvismania was alive and thriving in all its media-extended formats.

Having successfully "done" Elvis, it was commercially opportunistic to consider another American icon—Marilyn Monroe, second in fan adoration only to The King himself.

To fully exploit a biographical subject in all media, one needs the following ingredients: an iconic figure larger in death than in life, an anniversary date to launch the product (generally birth or death of sub-

ject), and—a necessary prerequisite—source or revelatory material that no one else has; that is, a raison
d'être for exploitation. As with Elvis, we had all three
with Marilyn.

Following the *Elvis* formula, we created the simultaneous media package of a television special, an 800
number, a book, and a video, all timed to the airing of
the show, all labeled with the same recognizable title.
If there was interest in *Marilyn,* there would be interest
in all the related *Marilyn Files* media products. It had
worked phenomenally well for *Elvis*; it should work
again for *Marilyn*. And it did.

We had repeated the same success formula, a total
barrage of related products, each one selling the other.
And we made sure we told the public "Brought to you
by the producers of *The Elvis Files*." We were saying,
in essence, that we knew how to do this and would
successfully create this media mix once again.

These examples serve to illustrate that sometimes
creative ideas just happen, and sometimes they are designed to happen. *Waldo* and Beanie Babies and
Chicken Soup just happened to materialize into an avalanche of assorted books, toys, calendars, and media
cottage industries with no discernable end in sight. *Elvis* and *Titanic* were orchestrated to be movies and
books and other products from their conception.

Today's media and merchandising opportunities have expanded far beyond the scope of a single product for a single medium. Book into film. Book into game. Toy into movie. Edutainment concepts into CD-ROMs. *Your* creative ideas can now become much more than what was initially designed for the printed page. The possibilities are limitless because information and creative concepts are now marketed and disseminated in a multiplicity of products. Where we were once inspired to read the book and see the movie, now we may also hear the song and buy the place mat. *Titanic* becomes *Titanic* mania—the movie, the song, the books, the lore.

Beanie Babies have become a cult phenomenon, and not so coincidentally, the exaggerated worth of individual Beanie Babies, disseminated through books and magazines, was primarily created by the manufacturers of the Beanie Babies—the Ty Toy Company. The now-legendary Harry Potter stories, by J. K. Rowling, have become a series of multimillion-copy bestselling books; a Warner Brothers movie; a merchandising bonanza of stick figures; and an array of toys and licensing paraphernalia.

If Beanie Babies have achieved cult status, Pokémon, inspired by Japanese animation and comics, has become a religion. Its now ubiquitous tag line—"Gotta

Catch 'Em All"—has spawned billions of dollars of licensing and merchandising sales across the world.

The Nintendo Game Boy Pokémon sales have extended into the millions; the animated TV show and the recent *Pokémon*—The First Movie (followed by The Second Movie) have captivated legions of adoring viewers. The obsession has engulfed multiple-format books from Scholastic, Golden Books, and Viz Communications. Over a thousand Pokémon merchandising products have been created and marketed, all emanating from the original Wizards of the Coast trading cards.

Imitators and media opportunists have joined the Pokémon craze. A female comic version—*Cardcaptor Sakura*—has become an animated television series. So has *The Sailor Moon. Princess Mononoke* is now the movie—and the companion books. Will this obsessive global merchandising phenomenon reach its ultimate saturation point? It hasn't yet.

Where do such ideas come from? How can *you* create the next Pokémon, Beanie Babies, Ninja Turtles, *Chicken Soup for the Soul*?

First step, visit the marketplace.

Your neighborhood bookstore, novelty shop, supermarket, game and toy store, newspapers, magazines, and television are all logical venues in which to conduct market research. Ask yourself what is trendy, cultist, and commercial at the moment. Why did some commercial products and current merchandising ideas succeed? Why did others fail? What worked? What didn't work? What might the public be interested in—now, next year, on some propitious anniversary? What nostalgia crazes of another era can be resurrected? What are possible future trends or cultist happenings? What significant events—like presidential elections, like the year 2001—will be absolutely certain to occur?

Studying current consumer trends is a mandatory exercise. Not for imitative reasons. Your market research is only meant to be a catalyst for perceiving why something like *Don't Sweat the Small Stuff* captivated a large, responsive national audience. Why did it work? What literary or creative idea can *you* conceive that could become a multitude of bestselling products? In essence, you are seeking the trendy topical subjects of next year—not an easy task.

What current fads and quirky ideas have captivated kids of this millennial generation? What is the buzz, the lingo, the hot trend that has begun to evoke regional or national attention? Whatever it is, it could become next year's bestselling group of products.

Someone will become rich and famous by finding

the next Barney or Beanie Babies. Someone will create the next Furby doll. It could be *you*.

As I've pointed out, creative ideas often emanate from or revolve around key anniversary dates and events—the fiftieth anniversary of Pearl Harbor, the twenty-fifth anniversary of the moon landing, the Olympics, presidential elections, the dawn of a new millennium, and celebrity birth or death dates. Our attention is media-saturated on these momentous occasions, and a receptive marketplace is primed to celebrate commemorative dates via the selective merchandise hawked and hyped *ad absurdum*. When Seinfeld left the airwaves, it was a fortuitous time to buy the scripts, wear the shirt, purchase the videos, collect all the memorabilia. That event would not come this way again soon.

Creative ideas also evolve from personal experiences and nostalgic memories. *Life's Little Instruction Book* by H. Jackson Brown Jr., published by Rutledge Hill Press in 1991, grew from a treasury of wise aphorisms handed down from father to son into a hugely bestselling series of books, calendars, posters, and other products. Barney was born out of a mother's desire to find a loving, wholesome, cuddly toy friend for her daughter.

Your childhood game or story or make-believe friend

could be the basis for an au courant media idea in today's market. The characters you create in the stories you tell your children could ultimately appear in books or on television or in electronic games. Or synergistic ideas could spring from your imagination. The now-immortalized Simpson family began life as a thirty-second vignette on the *Tracey Ullman* television show. The creator, Matt Gruening, had previously toiled and imagined the *Life from Hell* comic series in the counterculture newspaper *L.A. Weekly* for many years.

The idea for *Chicken Soup for the Soul* was turned down by over thirty mainstream New York publishers. "Too cute," they responded collectively. "Too sweet." In 1993 it was finally published by Health Communications, a small medical publishing house in Florida. Book number one led to *A Second Helping of Chicken Soup* and *A Third Serving of Chicken Soup* and then an entire industry of *Chicken Soup* for everyone. Over twenty-five million copies later, the authors are still marketing their idea and collecting an abundance of sweet stories and personal inspirational messages. The books have also become T-shirts and calendars, motivational tapes and inspirational workshops, and a weekly TV series. There has been more than enough *Chicken Soup* to go around.

The One-Minute Manager was a tiny self-published

morsel about becoming a more effective manager. The authors, Dr. Ken Blanchard and Dr. Spencer Johnson, applied their behavioral science and medical training backgrounds to helping people produce organizational and managerial results. They cleverly induced their own catalytic reaction by sending their small manuscript to hundreds of business leaders and executives in major corporations.

Their phenomenal little gem of a book was published nationally by William Morrow in 1981 and became an instant *New York Times* bestseller. In time, *The One-Minute Manager* begot *The One-Minute Parent, The One-Minute Salesman, The One-Minute Teacher,* a myriad of media products, and accolades and sales throughout the world.

A few years ago, an innovative media idea and mini-cottage industry came my way. Photos of the pop-cult legend Betty Page were brought to me by famed photographer Bunny Yeager. I didn't know who Betty Page was at the time but soon found out. Upon visiting the popular nostalgia comic book shops in Los Angeles, I quickly discovered that she was a 1950s icon, New York's Queen of Bondage, who disappeared into reclusion only to reemerge as a fictional character in *Rocketeer* magazine and become the cult fantasy of a new generation of college kids and nostalgia buffs. Her very photogenic face and body adorned posters, mugs, and calendars as a 1990s collectible.

Betty Page was the basis for an underground cult movement that spawned look-alike contests and an avalanche of collectors' memorabilia. With the celebrated Bunny Yeager photos as a centerpiece, I gathered research, wrote her bio, and solicited Buck Henry (who had written about Betty for *Playboy*) to write the introduction for a book. With a book package and presentation in hand, I found one of the few editors in New York publishing who knew who she was—the imaginative Jim Fitzgerald, then an editor at St. Martin's Press—and we effected a book publication deal. From there, our original Betty Page photos were extended into an eclectic assortment of media products—serialization to *Esquire* magazine, posters and calendars, a CD-ROM (*Betty Page—Highly Interactive*), and a pending television show. What started as a book concept (the original book is in its fifth printing to date) was exploited successfully into new products and new markets, each selling the others. Listed on each media product were bounce-back ads to buy the other Betty Page products. The key lesson here is to visualize, conceptualize—what *else* could your original product or idea become?

In 1999, a clever, quirky ad campaign was created for Taco Bell by the innovators at Chiat Day Agency. *"Yo quiero Taco Bell"* featured an endearing Chihuahua who captured our fancies and raised our spirits. It was so alluring, so delightful that it not only sold a lot of tacos and fajitas but became an instant licensing phenomenon that included T-shirts, hats, greeting cards, and posters, and maybe a book or more to be created down the line. *"Yo quiero Taco Bell"* soon segued into another popular ad cult expression—"Drop the *chalupa.*"

Often the vehicle or the medium becomes the trendsetting product. Page-a-Day Calendars, initiated by Workman Publishing, have become the mechanism through which all recent inspirational and motivational bestsellers are recreated as collections of aphorisms distributed over the 365 days of the year. Page-a-Days were the perfect vehicle for the likes of *Don't Sweat the Small Stuff* and *Life's Little Instruction Book,* and, of course, lots of *Chicken Soup.*

What is a similar commercial idea that has previously worked—yet is slightly different? What is "far-out" but within the mainstream of potential consumer interest and purchase? What will tomorrow's kids or tomorrow's teenagers ask, or demand, that their parents buy for them? Ask yourself, What else could my book, or screenplay, or idea become? How can I create from my original idea a mix of multimedia products that can be packaged for exploitation?

But first, last, and always, you must create and conceive the idea, the potential trend or commercially topical idea that could become the next media sensation. It may start out on the page, but it could become a major motion picture, a CD-ROM, a T-shirt, a doll, and much, much more. Never did John Gray, Ph.D., author of *Men Are from Mars, Women Are from Venus*, envision that his imaginative title would become a Mattel game. It has.

There are four essential questions that a book publisher, a film or TV producer, or other media purchaser will use as criteria for acquiring your creative idea or concept. They are:

1. What is it?
2. What is the appropriate marketplace?
3. Is it any good?
4. Is it commercial?

The first query relates to the treatment of the idea you have conceived. The second relates to its expected audience. For example, I have received many project submissions over the years that were proposed as books but in actuality were no more than magazine articles in their length and content. Other concepts that were oriented to movies and television may have been better suited for CD-ROM or video games. Some book-length products could inevitably be extended into ongoing series, hopefully similar in scope and success to the *Chicken Soup* phenomenon.

It is incumbent upon the creative writer to know

exactly what he or she has conceived—the right medium for each solicited endeavor.

You should initially ask yourself who your prototypical audience is. Is your idea geared to teenagers, or businessmen, or golfers, or a particular demographic or ethnic group? Who will buy your creative product?

Whether it is good and whether it is commercial are subjective judgments that most likely will be made by the media markets to which you submit. They will always be decision-making factors in the commercial evaluation of your book, screenplay, or project. It is probably the most important and ultimate criterion in deciding whether to acquire.

Describing specifically what you have created will naturally lead to writing it down on paper. This essential treatment, overview, premise, query—approximately two to twelve pages in length—is the key part of your presentation package. It will inform your targeted medium what your proposal is about, why you wrote it, and why your idea is commercially different from similar products on the market.

This treatment or overview will describe in depth exactly what your idea encompasses, the reason why you are offering this new creative project to a potentially receptive marketplace. It is your initial and perhaps your only opportunity to sell your idea. If it doesn't convey to the prospective buyer what you have in mind, it will not reach an audience. The length of the treatment is not as relevant as its focused content. What is unique about your idea? What are its commercial viability and potential? Who will buy it?

When my wife, Donna, a bestselling author in her own "write," conceived the presentation treatment with Dr. James Varni for their now-perennial bestseller *Time-Out for Toddlers,* the proposal was bought for the same reasons it was first turned down.

One major publisher rejected the proposal because it was "too niche a subject" in the burgeoning parenting book market: "Not broad enough in the disciplinary area."

It was bought for publication by Berkley Books because it focused "on a specific niche area in the parenting discipline area." The second publisher turned out to be a better prognosticator. *Time-Out* has sold over one hundred thousand copies to date.

The treatment/overview for a soon-to-wannabe major motion picture will often be synthesized down to tag lines or handles: "*Rocky* meets *Benji.*" "*The Big Chill* of the nineties." "*Friends* in a retirement home." Or as the legendary Dick Clark once told me, "Give it to me in a *TV Guide* blurb."

The Hollywood treatment—movie, TV, or cable—is invariably short and commercially succinct, loaded with handles and blurbs, as noted above. It consists entirely of simple, often simplistic, catch phrases intended to grab the prospective buyer. It alludes to something similar and previously successful, and it repeats a formula that has worked. Often, classics are reinvented in modern settings—familiar plots transformed into contemporary dramas or comedies. Thus *Romeo and Juliet* becomes *West Side Story*, Jane Austen's *Emma* segues into *Clueless*, and *Les Liaisons Dangereuses* becomes a New York teenage version called *Cruel Intentions*.

The Hollywood treatment is not subtle or subliminal. It is meant to titillate and evoke an immediate response. Plot and characters are revealed up front, and little is left to the imagination. This enables the head of development, the director, the producer, the VP of acquisitions to go to the moguls that be and condense it commercially into that *TV Guide* blurb. A sample of a movie treatment appears in chapter 6, and a TV treatment is in chapter 7.

When the original treatment/synopsis of the still-being-written *Message in a Bottle* was leaked to Hollywood, it already possessed all the formulaic ingredients that cried out for a sappy, soapy movie. It was reminiscent of *Bridges of Madison County* and *Love Story*, and it had box-office dollars attached to it. The movie-to-be was cast with Kevin Costner, Paul Newman, and Robin

Wright Penn about the same time the novel was being completed. The treatment had said it all.

The treatment for a film has to dwell, almost has to obsess, on plot and character. Character and plot. The subtle nuances, imagery, allegory, and ambient descriptions are generally left to the director, the auteur. But in recent Hollywood years, the once-forgotten writer has reemerged as an integral creative contributor to the movie and is more involved in the actual writing and scenic development after the plot has been purchased.

The treatment for the much-lauded screenplay and film *Thelma and Louise* was visual and visceral, and it evoked an emotional as well as a commercial response from the film producers who brought it to the screen. They knew there was something special and unique about this project.

Scripts and plot lines are often bought on a verbal pitch. So studio executives, development honchos, and producers unlimited are tuned into verbal pitch after verbal pitch without having to read a word on paper.

When I had discovered and was the proprietor of the number one national bestseller *And Ladies of the Club,* we offered the fifteen-hundred-page book to the movies via the motion picture offices of William Morris. After it had been submitted to a prominent producer, I inquired of our contact at the Morris Agency if the producer had read the book. She replied, "Read it? He had trouble getting through the treatment."

The business of turning treatments and plots into box-office gold was brilliantly satirized by Woody Allen in *Annie Hall*—the California segment. The creative writer at a Hollywood cocktail party is overheard lamenting, "Right now it's only a notion, but soon I hope to turn it into an idea and then a concept."

Everything in Lotus Land is *concept*, a well-conceived short description of a commercial film idea, or television series idea (e.g.—*Benji* meets *Rocky*—"Dog overcomes adversity and becomes a hero").

Your treatment or selling concept should necessarily allude to a media product that was previously successful but can be altered and done again. Similar—but different. If you've got the next *Blair Witch Project*, your idea will evoke immediate attention and response. If you've conceived the *Rocky* or *Godfather* of the "aughties" (the first decade of the new millennium), someone influential in the media will listen, and someone will buy—I'm confident of that.

The television industry requires broader, more detailed treatments and, again, that familiar formula.

But television has different formats, ranging from the miniseries and the MOW (Movie of the Week) to ongoing series—dramas, comedies, and the combined "drama-dies," which necessitate the creation of a pilot episode. A treatment geared to television must focus on the initial plot and story line that will hook the viewer, much like the famed opening murder scene in *The Fugitive* television show. The treatment will state the premise and unravel the plot: Once upon an earlier television time, a number of high-society people were stranded on an island in the Pacific. Thus were the beginnings of *Gilligan's Island,* which evolved into a long-running, unbelievably success-ful TV series. Each subsequent episode dealt with a differ-ent story that linked the characters indefinitely.

Another island—*Fantasy Island*—established the premise and setting of an array of fascinating guests who each week ventured onto the island to play out their fan-tasies. And in a similar formula, new guests set sail each week on the *Love Boat. Survivor* and *Big Brother* are cur-rent successful TV imports from England that are keyed to the serial concept of survival.

The TV series treatment begins with interesting char-acters in a certain milieu or setting who will interact with each other over the next thirteen weeks, if not longer. The treatment must delineate and detail the original set-ting—newsroom, ship, sorority, hospital—the players in the scene, the dilemma or the challenges confronting them, and the various ongoing stories that will pervade their lives and times each subsequent week. It is also necessary to describe each of the central characters (e.g., a perky young female news producer, a stiff and cur-mudgeonly anchorman, their irascible, tough guy boss) with all their idiosyncratic habits and gestures.

The MOW or miniseries treatment must pay heed to the longer length of the show. What will go into the two or four or six hours? How does the plot unravel over each hour each night? And how is action sustained and height-ened? The weekly series can be twenty-two or forty-four minutes in actual show time but not longer. Each story line fits that compact time allocation. But a more devel-oped plot must be concocted for a four-hour miniseries, running over two or three nights. Additionally, each hour must end at a pivotal time, with mini or maxi cliff-hangers. The formula is not unlike a Grisham, Ludlum, or Mary Higgins Clark novel, where each chapter com-pels you to read on to the next.

Television movie treatments will most likely be shorter than book treatments—more fast-paced, more episodic, with more emphasis on instant plot formulas and easy-to-stereotype but fascinating characters—and they will change and evolve just as soon as some young development whiz kid gets a notion to change them.

A friend of mine had written a lovely story treatment

about a young boy who found a treasure map hidden in Beverly Hills. When he returned from an in-person studio pitch meeting, he looked somewhat forlorn.

"Did they like it?" I asked expectantly.

"You know my little boy character?"

"Yes," I replied with enthusiasm.

"He's now a dog."

The treatment or overview for a fiction book proposal may be dependent on plot and characterization, but that is not germane for nonfiction subjects.

The nonfiction book treatment must relate very concisely to *why we need this book*. It has to sell the prospective editor, publishing house, and ultimately the consumer on the merits of the book. What makes your book different from other books on the market? Why would somebody want to buy it?

Assuming your book idea or book treatment concerns a universally appealing subject like diet or self-help or money, it must delineate exactly why the market would be responsive to yet another book on that subject. When we at Prentice-Hall discovered and acquired *Dr. Stillman's Quick Weight Loss Diet* (with some fifteen million copies now in print), the initial proposal featured salable ingredients that made it unique: *doctor* (medically sound), *quick* (instant results), *weight loss* (subject of infinite appeal). And it offered a gimmick—drinking an excessive amount of water each day. We published the book on the premise and promise of the book treatment and proposal. Its subsequent sales fulfilled the promise.

Al Secunda's *The 15 Second Principle* was originally entitled *Ultimate Performance* in its book proposal stage. It was turned down by numerous publishers because it did not stand out in the overcrowded self-help field. The book treatment was deemed not special or innovative enough to warrant publisher acquisition.

Al and I went back to the creative drawing board. We knew the subject matter would evoke a consumer response; we had to orient the proposal to reflect the uniqueness of this particular book. Again the key salient question had to be answered. Why did we *need* this book?

We conceived a title and blurb that would generate publisher awareness and enthusiasm, and the new book treatment reflected that premise. *The 15 Second Principle: Short, Simple Steps to Achieving Long-Term Goals* was submitted and soon purchased for publication by Berkley Books. It achieved bestseller status from the outset and garnered acclaim from such notables as Deepak Chopra, Jack Canfield (author of *Chicken Soup*), and astronaut Buzz Aldrin. A simple yet necessary adjustment to the book title and treatment made the difference between no publication and a very successful publication.

A nonfiction book proposal should be approximately

eight to twelve pages in length and double-spaced, and should be precise, original, and commercially descriptive of its subject. You must tell the publisher what is in your proposed book and why you are qualified to write it.

If you are conceiving a book treatment for a golf or tennis book and you have no credentials as a player or instructor, the solicited publisher may be skeptical about your credibility as an expert. Your expertise in the field you are writing about is a tangible asset in your book presentation.

Of course, there are exceptions, as evidenced by recent bestsellers like *Tuesdays with Morrie,* a poignant inspirational story about death—and about life—written by a sportswriter; and *Traveling Mercies,* a chronicle of faith written by novelist Anne Lamott. The important point is that your book presentation should be well developed and well elucidated. Your credentials, though meaningful, may be a secondary consideration.

Write about what you know, and make it interesting and enlightening. You are trying to evoke a response and are seeking publication. When I was president of Pinnacle Books, and author Elaine Partnow solicited me with her unique *Quotable Woman* presentation, I knew within the initial two pages that this was a significant candidate for book publication. The ultimate two-volume book series more than justified our faith in the potential of this special idea because it was established as a perennial seller and it was used in schools and colleges.

For children's, artistic, gift, and sometimes humor books, the treatment will necessarily have to be visual and should feature a simulated layout showing what the book will look like (often labeled a "dummy book"). This gives the publisher an opportunity to gauge the physical look and feel of the planned book. A visual book treatment is also required if the proposed book is to be elaborately designed (e.g., a cookbook, an exercise or photographic book). It is not mandatory for a basic nonfiction or fiction book.

The treatment/overview for a novel may describe the plot, the story line, and the essential characters, but almost invariably it must be accompanied by the full novel or a meaningful chunk. The publisher can only determine the worth and commercial viability of fiction by reading the book, not the plot synopsis alone. How the book is written is the essential element. Whereas Hollywood and television will buy on a plot outline and a pitch, the book industry generally needs to read a manuscript because that is what they will be publishing. There are no screenwriters or script doctors standing by to turn a notion, concept, or treatment into a finished product. The full presentation for manuscript submission consists of the book treatment or overview; an annotated table of contents (specifically outlining what will be in each chapter); an author biography; a comparison page or two showing how your book is different from similar books on the market; a marketing "bullet" sheet of the salient selling points, plus a sample chapter or two.

A *query letter* is different from a book proposal. It is written in letter format—no more than two pages—and asks the publisher or other medium to respond to the commercial merits of your idea. If the query letter titillates the prospective buyer, you will then be asked to send in a manuscript or a full proposal. At Pinnacle Books, and throughout my publishing career, I always responded favorably to a strong and interesting query letter.

The most intriguing book proposal I ever received was delivered in person. One afternoon my secretary buzzed me to say there was a man in the reception area who wanted to see the publisher. He announced that he was one of the three men on the grassy knoll who had assassinated President Kennedy and that he had a book proposal.

He *did* have a proposal, and I spent the next hour being absolutely mesmerized by his "true" account of the JFK assassination. It was vivid, incredible, and entirely plausible. He had been an integral part of contemporary history, so he attested, and he left me in awe, and with his treatment for the book-to-be. Eventually we declined the book—for reasons of incredulity and libel considerations. To my knowledge, his story was never published, but his tale remains plausibly speculative and intriguing to this day.

A treatment for solicitation to ancillary media (e.g., games, CD-ROMs, calendars) is different from that for a book or film presentation. It is far more concept-and idea-oriented. It must convey the idea clearly and succinctly and tell why it is geared to the specific market.

Why should your idea be converted into a game or greeting cards? What is unique about your concept that would translate into merchandise rather than a book or film? The "other media" treatment is more about the *why* than the *what*. It is less about plot, character, and annotated tables of contents and more about commercial merchandising and the branding and bundling of your idea.

Tell the potential buyer what your idea is, what the targeted audience is, and why your idea is or can be a commercial success—why it is unique. Start writing the concept or treatment based on sample movie, TV, or book treatments or on book jacket copy, on movie/TV promos, or commercial pitches that have worked before—and will work again. Make it quick and concise—about two or three pages in length.

A movie treatment may be transformed into a concept and ultimately, with some serendipity and the attachment of a marquee name or two, it could soon become a major motion picture. Dreams turned into ideas turned into treatments that are bought for book and screen— for fledgling writers, it's what bestseller and Hollywood dreams are made of.

It's said in Hollywood that if you experience a creative dream, you don't even tell the person you're sleeping with. Certainly if you conceive a commercial media idea, you don't discuss it in restaurants or public places. Such is the paranoia of the movie world, where ideas and dreams are stolen every day.

It's easy to steal ideas because many are developed in paragraph descriptions or *TV Guide* blurbs, as we noted in the previous chapter.

It's harder to steal a book since books are not hatched from a simple concept, but even this has been done.

So we are warned, implored, and advised to protect our sacred creative ideas, and we learn how to register, copyright, trademark, and patent. We may need the services of an attorney; we may do it ourselves. But we want to be sure that our original ideas are safely protected. We don't want to wake up one morning and read about or view something we once created that has been credited to someone else.

Sometimes we can't protect our ideas. Plots are lifted; concepts are stolen; literary creations are plagiarized. The quintessential Hollywood horror tale of recent years involves the now-celebrated *Art Buchwald* vs. *Paramount Pictures* lawsuit that captivated the film industry. Internationally beloved syndicated columnist Art Buchwald submitted an original idea to Paramount Pictures some years ago. The treatment and plot focused on an African head of state who came to America on an official visit and fell in love with a wife-to-be. It was based on a Buchwald-imagined political premise, turned into a full-fledged treatment, and offered to the marketplace via his film agent. Paramount optioned the property and offered a deal. They immediately saw it as a vehicle for their rising star Eddie Murphy, of *Saturday Night Live* and *Beverly Hills Cop* acclaim. The Buchwald "movie in development" was labeled *King for a Day.*

But *King* never had its day, at least not in its original incarnation. First it was put into "turnaround" (the opposite of "development"), and then it was dropped irrevocably. End of story—for a little while.

A few years later, a new blockbuster film emerged from the studios of Paramount, a star vehicle for their number one box-office performer, Eddie Murphy. It was called *Coming to America,* and it was about, familiarly, an African prince who comes to America and finds a bride. The film, produced for some $40 million, was a huge success and grossed over \$350 million worldwide. The story credit read "based on an idea by Eddie Murphy."

It all seemed too coincidental to Art Buchwald, his agent, and his attorneys—and they decided to sue Paramount Pictures and Eddie Murphy for blatantly stealing the idea/concept they had once bought from someone else—namely Art Buchwald.

The protracted litigation, over several years, changed the way Hollywood studios subsequently managed their creative accounting. The studio claimed that although the movie grossed nearly \$400 million, there were sadly *no* net profits. Buchwald and lawyers proved this to be mythical accounting and also won the case—proving that his original idea bought by Paramount had ultimately been stolen by Paramount. It was a Pyrrhic victory because the damages awarded only offset the legal costs of bringing the suit. However, Buchwald had won—he had proved his point.

Or, as some cynical Hollywood writer later said, "Imagine that kind of thing happening in this town."

Original concepts are "stolen" and "purloined" every day. People forget the source of their inspiration. Sometimes their muse is written material previously submitted to them, as was the case in the Buchwald-Murphy legal battle. An author of a book about the

Amistad slave ship rebellion sued Stephen Spielberg and Dreamworks for "lifting her created book material" for their movie. The case was ultimately settled out of court. Recently it was legally alleged that the innovative *Truman Show* film had plagiarized an Off-Broadway play with a similar theme and concept. But a more recent film—*EDTV*—also featured a very similar premise to that of *The Truman Show*. Are concepts copyrightable? Can ideas and original thoughts be protected? The answer is yes and no.

How do you protect yourself in Hollywood, where concepts and brief story lines are bought and sold on a regular basis? They are the lifeline of the industry.

You begin by sharing your most intimate creative ideas only with your intimates—if *they* can be trusted. In other words, let paranoia be your guide. Don't share your concepts, thoughts, or creative inspirations with anyone if you can help it.

Then do the following before proposing a movie or TV or live media project:

1. Register your treatment or idea or creative material (no matter what the length) with the Writers Guild of America West (WGAW), at 7000 West 3rd Street, Los Angeles, CA 90048, if you are West Coast–based, or the Writers

Guild of America East (WGAE), at 555 West 57th Street, New York, NY 10019, if you are based on the eastern seaboard. The cost is $20 per registration for nonmembers and $10 for members. Include with the payment one un-bound, loose-leaf copy of your material on 8½ × 11 standard white paper.

The cover sheet should state your title, full name, address, phone number, and social se-curity number. Your work will then be archived by the WGA Intellectual Property Registry, which will document your claim to authorship. Registrable material includes film or TV scripts, teleplays, treatments, outlines, manuscripts, novels, short stories, poems, lyrics, and draw-ings.

2. Send yourself and your attorney a registered let-ter stating the date when you completed your project and what it is about. When it is offered to the appropriate media, it will most likely come from an agent or lawyer who represents you. It is rare that Hollywood submissions are accepted from lay people or "nonpros" without formal industry representation. There have been Cinderella stories of manuscripts thrown into somebody's backyard or left "by accident"

on the desk of some bankable person who could say yes. But those are unusual, serendipitous happenstances, not the norm.

3. When your representative submits for you, he or she should send a formal cover letter that specifically states the date of submission, title and subject being transmitted, and author's name (you). Every record of submission, dated and annotated, is a step toward protecting your literary property. Of course, none of these steps would have prevented the Buchwald travesty. If some creative idea is going to be lifted or plagiarized, you usually cannot stop it before the fact. Such is the drama that has created a phalanx of Hollywood entertainment attorneys who make substantial livings from defending clients' properties and egos.

4. You and your agent or lawyer should keep copious records of the results of each submission: obviously who bought it—if that eventuates—but also all dates of rejection and from whom. Your record of solicitations is valuable for proof of ownership if that is needed later. The cover letters and the frenetic activity of registering and sending certified mail can also serve as a

deterrent to anyone contemplating theft of literary properties.

Remember, there are only ten to twenty basic plot formulas, so what's to prevent Paramount or Fox or MTV from saying, "We have that idea in development/in our files, under consideration, or on the drawing board"? Nothing. You will recall from a chapter ago how the writer's protagonist—a little boy—morphed into a dog in a single story conference. So whose concept was that—the guy who dreamed up the plot featuring a kid or the studio whose hero was a cute dog? And remember how the classic *Emma* became *Clueless,* a vehicle for Alicia Silverstone, without any credit or dollars accruing to Jane Austen (whose work in any case long ago entered the public domain).

The secret is to not give away too much of your idea, because then it's been heard around and it isn't your secret anymore. Just present enough to titillate the prospective buyer—and document that presentation. Then, upon a commitment, a small or large check advance, an option, or a formal letter of intent, you can divulge the middle, the ending, and the rest of the original plot or concept. You can further memorialize or substantiate this by attaching a screenplay of your project, or a character breakdown, or a detailed plot or scene breakdown.

Sometimes there *are* similarities that may or may not segue into legal jousting. Bestselling author Faye Kellerman recently claimed, in a copyright infringement suit, that the Academy Award–winning picture *Shakespeare in Love* was derived from her ten-year-old novel, *The Quality of Mercy*. Both creations contain similar plot elements—Shakespeare, the struggling young playwright in late-sixteenth-century England, falls in love with a damsel engaged to a nobleman. The lawsuit is directed at defendants Miramax, Universal Pictures, screenwriters Tom Stoppard and Marc Norman, and Hyperion Press, the publishers of the screenplay. Who is in the right, and who will win this copyright infringement suit? The courts will decide.

Scholastic, in tandem with Warner Bros., has filed a counter lawsuit against Nancy Stouffer on behalf of their celebrated author J. K. Rowling and her Harry Potter franchise. Stouffer legally claimed that the Potter series infringed her copyright and trademark rights by using Muggles characters, first introduced in her 1984 book, *Rah and the Muggles*. Scholastic's rebuttal is that the Potter books do not infringe on any right of Stouffer's.

You cannot register a book *idea*, and titles are not

copyrightable, but you can copyright an entire book. Write to the Copyright Office of the Library of Congress, Washington, DC 20559. Additionally, if a book is to be self-published, you can apply for an ISBN number through R. R. Bowker & Co. (the publishers of *Publishers Weekly* magazine) at 245 West 17th Street, New York, NY 10011.

Your book treatment or entire book, fiction or nonfiction, should be submitted under the auspices of a knowledgeable and reputable literary agent who has a proven track record in selling books (there are usually several in every large metropolitan city) or by an attorney. Reputable, because some are not; they just pretend to be. Knowledgeable, because your agent should know the major publishers and editors and be able to reach them. You don't want to sell to Boondoggle Press if your manuscript deserves Simon & Schuster. Again, every submission should be accompanied by a letter stating what and when you are submitting. After a response, favorable or unfavorable, document the result and the date. It is highly unlikely that bona fide publishers and their representative editors will steal your literary property.

Then there was the Jerzy Kosinski escapade. Kosinski's *Steps* was an internationally acclaimed, bestselling book. Some years back, a devilish young man in Los Angeles wanted to make a point. He retyped Kosinski's award-winning novel in manuscript format and submitted it as a first offering to some twenty-five publishers and agents. None of them recognized the work; most turned it down, saying that this kind of book was not in vogue; and only a small handful expressed any interest at all. Many points were obviously made in the process, including the stark reality that you can steal or borrow someone's property but you may not be able to resell it.

The key to book submission and protection is knowing where to send your material. Are they reputable publishers? Will they give you a response, and will they ultimately return your manuscript?

The big-name publishers will respect and honor your book submission. They are in business to publish the best and most commercial books they can acquire, not to steal anyone's material.

The cliché that imitation is the sincerest form of flattery often pervades the book industry. The euphemistic term is *derivative* books. The first *Joy of* title led to a host of *Joy of* imitators. The original *Everything You Always Wanted to Know About Sex* begat many successors. And the Wallace family's clever *Book of Lists* spawned a plethora of list publications, including

The Book of Sports Lists, which we "conceived" and published at Pinnacle.

Derivative books lead to more variations, sequels, and often a parody or two. In the never-ending business of *Chicken Soup for the Soul,* the imitators have included *Hot Chocolate for the Soul* and *Chocolate for a Lover's Heart. Don't Know Much About History* has led to *Don't Know Much About Geography* and *Don't Know Much About the Bible* by the same author, not to mention the many other derivatives.

It has been said that if you lift material from one book, it's plagiarism; if you borrow from many, it's research. You cannot prevent your creative writings from being borrowed or stolen once your book is published and disseminated to a mass public. You can protect your literary property before publication by overcompensating and adhering to the following guidelines.

1. Trademark (TM) your idea or intellectual property by writing to the Patent and Trademark Office, Washington, DC 20231, and, when found appropriate, applying for the appropriate trademark or patent. Their informational booklets will tell you how to apply and what to apply for.

Remember, the trademarking of your book- or creation-to-be is only necessary and possible if there is a catch phrase or slogan or new word coined that can lead to a series of books and ancillary product spin-offs. The *One-Minute Manager, Don't Sweat the Small Stuff,* and of course the legendary *Chicken Soup* are best-selling examples. *The 15 Second Principle* has acquired a trademark. You are, in essence, trademarking the franchise that may eventuate.

2. Copyright your book via the Copyright Office of the Library of Congress, 101 Independence Avenue, SE, Washington DC 20559. A copyright can only be granted for a tangible, physical, actual work that is to be distributed and disseminated in the marketplace, not for an idea or concept. We're trying here to distinguish between the publishing world and Hollywood. You can also secure a copyright for photos and visual materials.

The copyright notice appears in the following manner: copyright ©2001 Stan Corwin Productions.

Under current laws, a copyright lasts for the lifetime of the author plus fifty years. After that the work falls into the public domain.

Send your application for copyright by certified or registered mail, so you will have a record of receipt.

3. Maintain complete records and dates of all submissions and solicitations.

4. Send by registered letter confirmation of the receipt of your material. And send your material, when completed, to yourself as well, by registered letter for proof of mailing.

5. Know the market or publisher or media company to which you are submitting. Are they bona fide and legitimate? Are they listed in *Literary Marketplace, LMP,* and *Writer's Market*? Stay away from vanity press publishers, which charge you to publish your own book.

6. Don't tell too many people, particularly strangers or industry colleagues, about your creative or original ideas, unless they may be helpful to your literary endeavor.

7. Have an association with some media or literary attorney to whom you can refer and whose name, followed by Esquire, can be carbon-copied on your query or deal letters. The best recommendations for a literary attorney (or literary agent) should be sought from a writer or creator who has satisfactorily worked with him or her.

8. One final secret: Ideas and books are stolen more from novices and neophytes than from seasoned or published authors. If you have prior credits, list them to indicate your track record and your previous successes. If I were presenting this book, I might write:

THE CREATIVE WRITER'S COMPANION
by Stanley J. Corwin

Author of *How to Become a Bestselling Author*

If you are creating for the electronic media or for Internet games or CD-ROMs, it might be appropriate for you to acquire a patent in addition to or in lieu of a trademark or copyright. For more information about patents, write to the U.S. Patent and Trademark Office, Washington, DC 20231. You will likely have to submit blueprints and/or diagrams along with your patent proposal.

Since the burgeoning electronic field is so innovative and is changing so rapidly, it is best to be cautious about your foray into these new media ventures and to have a knowledgeable attorney on your side. Your printed creative work is easier to protect and police than an electronic translation appearing in another language, in another country. You can only follow the guidelines recommended in this chapter and hope an electronic rendition of your creation does not materialize without authorization in Sri Lanka. And if it does, you should be flattered.

Once upon a time, several decades ago, the standard publisher's contract claimed all rights (for the publisher, not the author) "not specifically enumerated" that were "hereinafter coming into existence."

The basic ancillary rights markets then included print excerpt, book club, movies, television, dramatic, and foreign translations. Those rights yet to be discovered turned out to be more commercially viable than anyone ever imagined.

In the 1980s and 1990s a burgeoning and exploitative new media world emerged in the forms and formats of book audiotapes, CD-ROMs, electronic games, videos, Internet rights, and mass merchandising. Where published books were once sold only to markets like the Literary Guild or *Esquire* magazine or for feature motion pictures, there were now exciting new media markets to exploit.

Where once a subsidiary rights sale of a book was made to a book club or a magazine, today's potential and lucrative markets are infinitely more expansive.

A bestseller, particularly by a brand-name author like Stephen King or Andrew Weil, may be resold and reconfigured into media products like desk calendars, CD-ROMs, Internet chat rooms, audiotapes, and other merchandising. Bestselling novels may be sold to audio and film markets and publishing licensees throughout the world.

Ragtime by E. L. Doctorow emerged over a number of years as a successful film and a Broadway musical. Ken Burns's *Civil War* was a coffee-table book and a groundbreaking TV documentary series. Pokémon began life as Japanese animation, then exploded around the world into every media configuration imaginable.

The cliché "If you loved the book, see the movie" could be reinvented today as "If you loved the book, see the cable special, listen to the tape, play the electronic game, and put the calendar on your desk." Books and creative written ideas have been turned into a host of interesting media products.

Two publishing industry innovators—John McMeel, chairman and founder of Andrews McMeel and Universal Press Syndicate, and Peter Workman, chairman and founder of his eponymous publishing house, Workman Publishing—were in the forefront of the ancillary products explosion. McMeel realized a few decades ago that the popular syndicated comic strips he published could be exploited as a mass configuration of media merchandising products. *Calvin & Hobbes, The Far Side, Ziggy,* and *Cathy* also became calendars, place mats, greeting cards, and mugs because they were immediately recognizable to the legions of comic strip devotees who grew up with them.

Peter Workman pioneered the "Page a Day" calendars as a book by-product and turned it into a burgeoning cottage industry. His many other unique and quirky book ideas also transcended other media and merchandising markets, including the bestselling book series that began with *What to Expect When You're Expecting*.

There are now more commercial opportunities than ever for original creative ideas to be exploited in the electronic, digital, and merchandising worlds, as well as in print. You have to know what you have created and what it can potentially become. Novels rarely become calendars and place mats. Books on golf do not become TV miniseries. But books on golf, like Harvey Penick's bestselling gems, have become audiotapes and desk calendars.

In my popular UCLA course, "Selling Your Creative Ideas to All Media" (the inspiration for this book), the attendees came from a variety of professional fields. There were doctors and lawyers, actors and actresses, an insurance salesman, a singer, a dog trainer. But they shared a commonality of creative ideas and yearnings. They each had a single idea, and it was generally geared to one particular medium. One had a screenplay. Another had an idea for a children's series. Another was inventing a game.

Could the game also be a book or a CD-ROM, like *Myst* or *Clue*? Could the children's series be filmed? Could a line of stuffed or electronic toys evolve from the characters?

We started to talk and think multimedia. How could their individual creative ideas be exploited in various multimedia configurations? I had to tell them what was out there. I had to share with them what "they" were buying. This book is the first to discuss and explore every potential market for media exploitation.

Acclaimed screenwriter William Goldman remarked some years back that "in Hollywood, no one knows anything." The "they" in Hollywood, New York book circles, and the rest of the media and merchandising world is a generic, amorphous being. There is no one arbiter, scientific wizard, or prognosticator who *knows* what the next hit or exploding trend will be. If one person did, he or she would be made president of ABC or Random House or Paramount Pictures tomorrow. The hits are often based on a guess, sometimes spontaneous and impulsive, sometimes "experienced intuition."

So *your* creative idea may be turned down again and again—like *Chicken Soup* or *Forrest Gump* or even *Star Wars*—not on the basis of any particular insight or empirical criteria. You should never be deterred by anyone's rejection or subjective decision. "They" don't really know what the next bestseller or blockbuster film will be. No one does. You must keep trying if you truly believe in your idea or project.

The first Beanie Babies or the first *Don't Sweat the Small Stuff* can break out, but the successor imitators may never materialize commercially. The first may have been timely and unique, and it may have been enough to satiate the marketplace. The buyers of media ideas have to guess *when* as well as *what*. Timing is crucial, and word of mouth can be contagious.

At recent Book Expo national conventions, where every forthcoming book, calendar, and merchandising item is on display, there have been discernable trends. Any successful generic idea has become immediately "franchisable." So *Chicken Soup for the Soul* not only dished out more helpings but segued into an entire industry. There emerged a *Dummies' Guide* and an *Idiot's Guide* for every conceivable subject. Both popular series were parodied together in Ten Speed Press's imaginative lampoon *The Dummies' Guide for Idiots*.

Don't Sweat the Small Stuff was spun into additional titles for the home and the office, into mini inspirational books for Mother's Day and Father's Day, and beyond. Frederick Fell Publishers began the *Know It All* series. The bestseller *Spontaneous Healing* became an ongoing series of spin-off books. *The Seat of the Soul* led to *Soul Stories*.

Publishers repeated the motion picture industry formula of sequelizing a success. Give the public the same success, but change the formula ever so slightly. Following this truism, George Lucas certainly gave them what they wanted—the *Star Wars* "prequel"—the beginnings of a galaxy far away and long ago. And the flood of books and merchandise products included novelizations, coloring and sticker books, posters, calendars, games, cups, and blueprints. Everyone got in on the *Star Wars* licensing because it was prehyped and presold. It couldn't miss commercially.

When Pokémon, the electronic video game craze, was exported to the world from Japan, it quickly became a mega-selling series of books, comics, videos, graphic novels, trading cards, a TV show, a Web site, and now, a very major worldwide motion picture. Like its instant fad predecessors—Teletubbies, Tamagotchi, and Beanie Babies—it hit on all products, and the merchandising boom proliferated into a billion-dollar business of exploitative media items. The obsessed and generally young fanatic wanted all the products. They had become collectible.

Often, book-driven products begin their media lives as projected series. Bestselling examples include *The Baby-Sitters Club* and *Goosebumps,* which were designed as ongoing book series for young people. They soon exploited their way into other media but oversaturated a marketplace that couldn't absorb their productivity.

Sometimes an idea has an altruistic origin. *Life's Little Instruction Book* originated as a collection of inspiring messages and homilies that a father put in writing for his son. And they grew into a little book of wisdom that was published by a small company, Rutledge Books, in Nashville, Tennessee. No one ever planned or expected that it would sell millions of copies and become a perennial bestseller. Of course it led to sequels, but many imitative versions rushed to the market by other publishers were less successful.

The huge bestseller *The 7 Habits of Highly Successful People* spawned many derivative books fixated on that number—books titled 7 *Things* . . . or 7 *Ways* . . . proliferated. *Men Are from Mars, Women Are from Venus* inspired a frenzy of similar wordplay titles, most of them unsuccessful.

The transition from one medium to another does

not guarantee success. It often means a different audience, and the new media product may not be as good. The popular *X Files* TV show didn't translate commercially when it came to the big screen as a feature motion picture. Nor did the books sell in numbers commensurate with the popularity of the television series. The remake of the classic *Avengers* TV show as a film was a disaster at the box office. Similarly, the 1990s movie version of *Godzilla* had dismal results commercially, and its merchandising by-products crashed with it. No one wanted to see the movie, buy the book, or collect the action figures.

X Men languished as a cult comic book series, but found new life as a box-office film bonanza.

Buffy the Vampire Slayer failed as an original movie initially but appealed to enough of a cult audience to be revived as a very popular television series. It found additional new life as a book series and other ancillary merchandise. No one would bet against a second attempt at a major motion picture. The cycle could come around again.

The media markets—in all of their guises and disguises—tend to replicate what has been successful, what has worked before. They are often cautiously slow to innovate. Many of the rejections and turndowns you will receive for your new concept or idea will invariably read "We've never done this," "It's not for us," "We're not sure how to market this," or "It's not what they're buying."

How do "they" know? They don't. They are only guessing about the next commercial trend, just like everybody else.

On a number of occasions I have received a rejection letter for a creative, original idea that stated, "This is very well-done and very commercial, *but not for us.*" Why wouldn't it be for them? I always feel like returning the letter and writing on the bottom, "Then for whom?"

The paradox of bestselling hits is that no one knows they will be a hit until it happens, and then everyone wants to jump on the imitative bandwagon. No one wanted any *Chicken Soup*. Now they want any inspirational tale that resembles it—until the next trend surfaces and captivates our attention and pocketbook. What can we, the creators, do to anticipate and discover the next media blockbuster?

We can assiduously study all the media and merchandising empirical data over recent years. We can learn what worked—and what didn't. What media products captured the whim of the public? Why did they? What worked for adults—of what age? What did children, or teens, love or obsess over?

In an unknown, uncharted area, where *you* are the first, *you* are the innovator, you have to believe very fervently in your idea, and you have to guess that your time is right now.

When I discovered *And Ladies of the Club,* the work of Helen Santmyer, an eighty-eight-year-old woman in an Ohio nursing home who had been writing her novel over fifty years, I guessed that the time and the market were ready for a fifteen-hundred-page epic novel that encompassed a century of American life. It meant going against the grain of the quickie pop commercial novels that everyone was reading. Maybe it was time for one of those "old-fashioned" novels, the kind Dreiser or Henry James used to write. My intuitive guess worked out: *Ladies* appealed to the American public, became a number one bestseller, and has sold (to date) over four million copies.

The media marketplace today consists of the traditional buyers—book publishers, movies, television, print media, book clubs, foreign buyers—and a brand-new electronic mix of new markets—the Internet, CD-ROM, audio, digital and educational software, games, video, merchandising outlets that include calendars, posters, bookmarks, mouse pads, greeting cards, place mats, toys, stickers, and more. There are also "special sales" markets, where books and media products are geared to corporate buyers, gift purchases, or special imprint sales. Your creative idea may forego the familiar sales route via retail stores and be designed as a personally imprinted or custom-made product for a large company or organization.

You must know exactly what you have created and how it fits into a potential media marketplace. And invariably you will have to educate that marketplace. The buyers ("they") are comfortable with formulaic ideas and projects, with what they know and what they've sold and disseminated before. If you are offering a new concept, you will have to provide meaningful insights into *how* and *why* it will work commercially. Why will someone buy your idea? Why do they need it?

Show your buyer how to market it—and be very specific. After you've protected your idea, try it out in focus groups, with a test audience, with children's classes, with a random sampling. Then you can entice your potential media acquirer by showing the results. The first kids' audience loved Barney, and so ultimately (not so surprisingly) did everyone else. Don't give up. Your deal may materialize on the first, third, or twenty-eighth solicitation. If you believe it will happen, and your belief is based on cogent assumptions rather than just hype and hope, then it will happen—sometime, hopefully sooner than later. Timing is most significant in the creative selling process. So is luck. As the sage philosopher and legendary football coach Vince Lombardi once said, "Luck is when opportunity meets preparation."

In my early book-publishing years, I was a young licensing VP at Grosset & Dunlap. We were the publishers of the classic young people's series *Nancy Drew* and *The Hardy Boys*—every child's growing up stories. The myriad number of continuing volumes sold hundreds of thousands of copies perennially through retail bookstores. But then a unique venture came my way.

A close friend of mine was a marketing innovator, packaging and selling merchandisable products and premiums to major brand-name companies like Proctor & Gamble, Lipton, and Pepsi-Cola. Over lunch one day, we discovered that I represented America's favorite stories of our youth and he represented a colossal client—Post Cereals—that sold to those kids. Well, the wheels and deals clicked, and the timing was propitious. To condense the longer story of effecting a licensing agreement, we arranged the placement of ads on twenty million boxes of Post Raisin Bran offering "Your First Starter Set" of *Nancy Drew* and/or *The Hardy Boys*.

The campaign achieved extraordinary results. The immediate benefits were twofold—Post Raisin Bran sold over one million copies of Grosset's *Nancy Drew* and *Hardy Boys* series, and the national advertising blitz generated additional sales and interest in the on-going series.

We had created crossover sales by combining two unlikely markets; cereal boxes were not an obvious sales arena for the merchandising of books. It was creative, innovative marketing that worked, and it taught me the lasting lesson that no venture or unusual product marketing is impossible—certainly not because it has never been tried before. Someone has to be first.

As we move into the new millennium, creative ideas and works will find new markets of opportunity and commercial exploitation.

Book products will not only be printed and published but downloaded and uplinked via the computer and the Internet. They will begin as traditional books and then be reconfigured as other electronic and physical mass products. Media ideas will emerge via the vast extensions of the Internet and the global reaches of the electronic world.

It is important that *you,* the creator, read and study all the latest media and electronic trends and innovations. Clip articles, do research, and save data that may pertain to your creative and commercial interests. You may discover a new media product, a new medium, or a franchisable merchandising opportunity. It is happening every day—at an accelerated pace.

If you are a writer and creator, there will be greater possibilities to sell your ideas. Where once only a few media markets existed, new arenas of media development and exploitation now seem to be discovered every month. Your media concept can be much more than a book or a game or a calendar. It can be conceived and packaged with multiple markets in mind. Your idea could be the next Harry Potter or *Chicken Soup* or *Star Wars*. It will depend on the creative strength of your concept, its sales and marketing prospects, and the ability of the initial media buyer to perceive what it is and commit to it financially. It may depend on your educating that buyer—and on that certain element of luck, when *your* opportunity meets *your* preparation.

Before globalization and megamedia dominance, there once was an enclave of middle-sized, individualistic, creative publishers that flourished over decades, sometimes centuries. They included Macmillan, Bobbs Merrill, Grosset & Dunlap, Atheneum, Dodd Mead, Viking, and many others. They now exist (if they still exist at all) as editorial imprints of larger publishing companies and conglomerates.

In the 1980s and 1990s, the global and national media behemoths unleashed a barrage of corporate acquisitions. Viacom (already owners of Paramount Pictures, MTV, and Blockbuster Video) bought Simon & Schuster. They have since announced that they will be adding the CBS network to their corporate portfolio. Rupert Murdoch's News Corporation acquired HarperCollins, which in turn absorbed William Morrow and Avon Publishers, formerly part of Hearst. Pearson Penguin, out of England, purchased Putnam Publishing, which had become an amalgam of what was once Berkley Books, Jove, Tarcher, Price Stern Sloan, and Grosset & Dunlap. Von Holtzbrinck, from Germany, was the new owner of an American publishing combine of St. Martin's Press, Farrar Straus, and Henry Holt.

An even larger German media conglomerate—Bertelsmann—soon engulfed the once individual and venerable American publishers Random House, Knopf, Ballantine, Crown, Villard, Bantam, Doubleday, and Dell. The distinct publishing names of Bantam and Dell soon assimilated into BantamDell.

Where thirty to forty reputable New York houses once published independently, only a dozen now dominated the business in the twenty-first century. Approximately 90 percent of the *New York Times* bestseller list was controlled by this elite faction. The New York publishing scene had been merged and submerged into a global conglomerate structure. The primary publishing world had changed and been reconfigured. It was sad for some—emerging authors, agents, employees—and beneficial for others—deal makers, film companies, licensers of brand names.

The encouraging publishing news was emerging from the hinterlands, where small and medium-sized publishers were being born and thriving. For the neophyte author, new markets of specialty publishing houses were now looking for potentially commercial manuscripts.

Outstanding regionally based publishers now existed—Andrews McMeel in Kansas City, Running Press in Philadelphia, Peachtree in Atlanta, New Horizon in Far Hills, New Jersey, Ten Speed in Berkeley, California, and Adams in Holbrook, Massachusetts. Niche market publishers like Conari Press and The Crossing Press (New Age and women's issues), HCI (the life issues and *Chicken Soup* for everyone publishers), Meadowbrook for children's publications, and Klutz for games and recreational hobbies were all successful and expanding at an appreciable rate.

There were now perhaps more—but different kinds of—companies that could successfully publish specialized books, catapult them to bestseller status, and exploit them in ancillary media and merchandising markets.

The conglomerate houses focused on bestsellers and brand-name authors in hardcover and paperback formats. Although they paid big bucks for the privilege, they were usually guaranteed commercial success by such names as Stephen King, Danielle Steel, Mary Higgins Clark, Tom Clancy, and John Grisham. Additionally, they published commercial nonfiction in almost every special category: parenting, health, self-improvement, finance, fitness, spirituality, and more.

They were editorially and promotionally geared to the potential bestseller and the perennial seller that could endure on their backlist.

Franchisable books like *Chicken Soup* and *Dummies* and *Don't Sweat the Small Stuff* could be sequelized ad infinitum. Books like *What Color Is Your Parachute?* and *The Guinness Book of World Records* could be annualized. The popular trade paperback format emerged as a viable one for literary fiction and for handy quick-help nonfiction.

Because the retail markets had expanded to superstores, price clubs, and on-line outlets, there were greater opportunities to reach and sell books to the public. The Internet made backlist books a favorable commodity—worth keeping in print and available to the public. Publishers did not have to maintain large quantities in stock, and they could print on demand or have a book downloaded in response to a specific customer order. (Much more to come on this vital new marketplace in chapter 10.)

Reading Clubs also proliferated across the country for favored and contemporary literary works, many spawned as Oprah (Winfrey) Book Club selections. Literary discussion groups featuring finer trade paperback novels like *The Reader, Enduring Love,* and *The*

Poisonwood Bible became popular in both large cities and small regional enclaves.

The niche, regional, and mainstream publishers all had to qualify and control their publication output in vying for shelf and on-line selling space. They had to be selective about what they published, and attuned to the market competition. It was simultaneously incumbent upon creators or authors to be knowledgeable about the marketplace and to envision the format and promotional appeal of their potential books. The soliciting author had to favorably satisfy the answer to the publisher's inevitable question—"Why should we publish this book?"

There were now other variables and considerations in purchasing a book for publication. Was the author promotable and/or mediagenic enough to make television appearances? Did he or she have any professional sales markets that could be solicited apart from the retail sector? What other product or ancillary markets could be exploited to extend this book as other merchandise? In other words, could the book be more than a book?

In some instances, book publication might follow a successful launch in another media area. *Dilbert* and *X Men* were initially comic strips, Barney a toy, and

Austin Powers a movie. *South Park* was a television show that begat a cottage industry that segued into book titles. Sometimes you might be selling a single title, sometimes a series or franchisable concept, and sometimes a potential configuration of media merchandise. The publisher was not only asking, "Is this publishable? Is this commercial?" but "What else could this idea be?"

Your book idea would find a responsive publisher if you chose a universally appealing subject—diet, making money, living longer, being fulfilled—but if it was not commercially unique or different from its competitors, it would saturate an already oversaturated marketplace. It had to be the *same*—but *different*. There had to be a compelling reason for it to be published, and bought. It had to have commercial potential for both the front list and the backlist.

The "bestseller" houses want what will sell, want their market share of brand names, and want what is topically and commercially relevant. When millions of people are mesmerized by TV saturation of the lives of O.J. and Monica and Princess Diana, the publisher has a built-in audience—but has to guess when the hype and the product demand will end. No one cared about the memoirs of Johnny Cochran, Marcia Clark, or Paula Barbieri. We had seen and heard enough. There was nothing revelatory left to sell. Books tied to the movie of *The Postman, End of Days,* and *Seven Years in Tibet* didn't sell because the movies didn't sell. We didn't need to read about what we didn't want to see.

The major houses have the media clout and the money to hype the latest bestseller-to-be. But hype often backfires. Overhyped autobiographies by Whoopi Goldberg and Dick Morris failed to achieve sustained sales. Books on the imminent Y2K crisis proliferated but generally remained unsold. Too many were published, and their apocalyptic pronouncements didn't titillate us; we waited to see what would eventuate.

When ideas or new book ventures are brought to me, as they constantly are, I ask myself and I ask the neophyte author, "Why do we need this book? Why do we need another book on this subject?" As authors we must confront the question to our own and to the potential publisher's satisfaction.

The Betty Page Scrapbook was the first mass market book on this popular cult figure, although a myriad of other similar merchandising products had enjoyed considerable success. Diane Stein's book on Reiki (Crossing Press) popularized a subject that had previously received little print attention, and this outstanding book has sold over 150,000 copies to date. *Attitudes of*

Gratitude was a cleverly conceived Conari Press title with a message, and it sold consistently well in its initial and sequel editions. The timing was extraordinarily opportune.

Your idea may be the first, or the last, but it must be the best and the most enduring, and be the right book, for the right market, at the right time.

After you've protected, registered, and copyrighted your book idea, it is essential that you research the most compatible publisher for your particular project. Your friendly neighborhood bookstore is generally the best place to ascertain who is publishing in your field.

The New York–based publishers have the most sales and promotional clout in launching a potential bestseller. These majors include Random House, Knopf, Crown, Villard, Ballantine, BantamDell, Doubleday Broadway within one publishing conglomerate, and Penguin Putnam, Simon & Schuster (with Scribners), HarperCollins, (now aligned with Morrow and Avon), St. Martin's Press, Henry Holt, and Farrar Straus and Giroux (in the same corporate family), Harcourt, Houghton Mifflin, Warner/Little, Brown, and remaining independent houses like Norton and Workman. If your book landed with one of these publishers, you would likely enjoy a bigger advance, more promotional effort, and a larger initial distribution.

The specialty and niche publishers are good in the areas in which they publish. If your book focuses on career opportunities or self-help subjects, Ten Speed Press or Adams are likely publisher candidates. The aforementioned Workman Publishers and Andrews McMeel specialize in humor; Meadowbrook for parenting books; HCI and Avery in the health field; Conari Press and The Crossing Press for women's issues. And there are smaller but excellent niche publishers like Lone Eagle and Michael Wiese that concentrate on film titles. All have acceptance and credibility at the retail buying level because they have proven track records in these specialty fields.

There is no doubt that the mega bookstore chains—Barnes & Noble and Borders—the price clubs like Sam's and Costco, and the on-line colossus Amazon.com will control the quantity purchases of books in this country in the foreseeable future. Their buy-ins influence the sales and bestseller status of both new booksand brand names. Their displays and promotion—end caps (minirack and shelves at the end of an aisle), counter and floor displays, readings, book signings—are all effective means of attracting buyers. If a book benefits synergistically from cross-merchandising with other same-title media products, the bandwagon effect heightens consumer attention and generates sales. Deepak Chopra's bestselling books are being sold in concert with his journals, calendars, recordings, audiotapes, and even herbal supplements. Stephen Spielberg's film version of Arthur Golden's celebrated bestseller, *Memoirs of a Geisha,* will be accompanied by licensed beauty and fashion products with an Asian theme.

When you submit your creative idea as a book presentation, the package must include a *query letter* explaining why you wrote this book, why there is a market need for it, and who you are professionally. Additionally, the heart of your presentation will be the *book proposal,* consisting of an overview of the contents of your prospective book, an annotated table of contents (not just a listing), a sample chapter or two, a market comparison to other books in this field or genre (and why yours is different), and a full author biography. And, as noted earlier and often, tell your publisher-to-be what other media or merchandising product your book already is—or can be.

Assuming that your book proposal is now going to the appropriate publisher in its field, it is equally necessary to send it to the appropriate editor. You can't just send it to HarperCollins. It will either sit in a manuscript pile, remain unopened, or—perish the thought—be thrown out. Through friends, contacts, other writers, the pages of *Literary Marketplace* or *Writer's Market*, or a phone call or two to that house, you can find out the name of a key person and send your presentation to either the publisher, the editor-in-chief, the executive editor, the managing editor, or someone of similar editorial rank and title. Of course, your submission may come from your agent, if you have one, who will most likely know these editors.

I'm reminded of the time when I was a young rights director at Prentice-Hall and we submitted our new books for excerpting to a West Coast magazine. The solicitations invariably went to the various names on the masthead—the executive editor, the managing editor, and so on. On an initial trip to the Coast, I called on the publisher and asked to meet the editors with whom I was frequently corresponding. Not to be found. Not to be met. They didn't exist. They were fictitious names on the masthead, all a pseudonymous invention of the *only* editor, the man I had just met. Be sure, if you can, that you are submitting your magnum opus to a *real* person. It will greatly facilitate a publication response.

Many *real* editors can make a difference in your quest for bestsellerdom. They have clout in their own shops, they retain respectability in the marketplace, and they have successfully guided your kind of book to publication before. Some of these editors have their own imprint within the publishing house. Some have "discovered" acclaimed bestsellers and are able to sustain that reputation for a while.

Your book may also be adaptable to foreign markets, depending on the subject. What will translate—literally and figuratively—into Spanish, French, Japanese, and other languages is often speculative and not obvious. In general, the big bestsellers in all Western countries also find markets across the oceans. Helen Santmyer's *And Ladies of the Club* was translated into some five languages. All the foreign volumes shared one commonality; they were a thousand pages plus in thickness.

These digital days, and with the Internet engulfing our lives, the "self" and "virtual vanity" publishers are growing at an extraordinary rate. You are now able to write your own book, make it available on your own Web site, provide a downloadable copy on demand, and bill the purchaser directly. No publication contract, no production process, no distribution, no returns. Instant sales results. And if you were diligently ambitious, you could link up to Amazon or Barnes & Noble on-line for traditional sales.

A likely scenario that may evolve is when brand names like John Grisham or Stephen King or Mary

Higgins Clark bypass his or her publisher, bypass the retail bookstore and normal book distribution, and announce their next book on the Internet. Since it is generally a much-heralded event-in-waiting, the legions of devotees flock to his Web site to purchase their own special copies, perhaps signed by the author. Again—the fantasy of no distribution costs, no overzealous printings, no returns. Just sales on demand. Prior to that possible scenario, Stephen King made his novella *Riding the Bullet,* available via the Internet and some 500,000 devotees downloaded it within a week. He has continued this concept with a new Internet novella. Grisham is publishing a current novel—*A Painted House*—in serial format in *The Oxford American,* a bimonthly literary magazine of which he is publisher and owner.

You wouldn't generate the same results for *your* first novel or first book, but you have the prospect of bundling other merchandise to sell on your site—calendars, stationery, greeting cards, audiotapes, whatever—if and when they are merchandisably suitable. If you are pursuing the traditional publishing route, remember to tell your prospective publisher how you might exploit your book in other media and merchandising formats. The synergy of book into film into ancillary products will create greater recognition and sales opportunities for the original product. *Read* the book, *see* the movie, *hear* the tape, *wear* the sweatshirt has become more of a merchandising norm than a rare occurrence.

An attention-getting query letter that will most likely motivate a response from your selected editor could read as follows:

Dear Ms. or Mr. Editor:

I am a nationally visible marriage and family therapist based in Santa Barbara, California. I write a monthly column for *Marriage* magazine, and I have a popular Web site that is linked to *iVillage*.com. I have appeared on numerous television talk shows including *Leeza, Rosie O'Donnell,* and *Dateline.* I am the author of *Same Wife, Separate Life*—Euphoria Press, 1996.

I enclose a book proposal and sample chapter of my new manuscript—*My Husband Is Not My Daddy: A Woman's Guide to Relationships.*

I think you will find this refreshing and unique, framing a new, modernistic approach to the subject of male-female relationships. I am planning to develop and exploit this project as a

TV documentary, audiotape, and series of Internet and live seminars, as well as a book.

I will look forward to your response.

Sincerely,
Prospective Author

This is a great prototypical letter to an editor because it contains all the buzzwords that titillate an editor and a publishing house.

It covers all the bestseller ingredients—the author's credentials, the appealing title and subject, the promotional opportunities, and the likelihood of expanding media and merchandising exploitation. It will probably evoke a favorable response from the editor *if* the accompanying book presentation fulfills the editorial premise and promise. It touches all the ancillary bases.

The book proposal should be unique—*and* commercial. Your title and accompanying subtitle or blurb (if nonfiction) are a significant factor in eliciting publisher interest. They were certainly a determining variable in the acquisition of such inevitable bestsellers as *The Gifts of the Jews: What Western Civilization Owes an Ancient Nomadic Tribe, Every Day's a Party:*

Recipes for Cooking Louisiana Style, and *Who Moved My Cheese?: An Amazing Way to Deal with Change in Your Work and in Your Life*.

For nonfiction book proposals, your objective is to sell either a different approach to a familiar commercial category or a revelational, groundbreaking new idea. With fiction (where you may have to submit the complete novel), the publishing decision is determined by the commercial appeal of the plot and the quality or appeal of the writing.

Most proposals are rejected because the prospective authors didn't do their homework. Reasons may include sending it to the wrong publisher, not establishing a market or niche need, an unappealing title and blurb, a poorly defined table of contents, and an unconvincing or uninspired overview. There is a myriad of reasons for rejection, but a strong proposal that substantiates the uniqueness and commercial potential of the book concept will be bought for publication more often than not.

The neophyte author should study the book formulas and concepts that have worked. Read the jacket blurbs and promotional copy. Why did they appeal to the reader and buyer? What were the unique ingredients that merited publication and perhaps helped to create success or bestselling sales? Be cognizant of titles and subtitles and the very specific selling handles that titillate the consumer. Know the publishers in your field or genre—the ones that have achieved success and the ones that haven't.

Your book may be a national bestseller, a franchisable series or sequel, or a one-time publishing experience. It is greatly dependent on luck, timing, and exploitative opportunities. There is a whole new media world out there ready to be exploited for the right commercial media or book property. Your job is to create that property at the propitious time and know how to market it.

Book into film is generally a rare happening. And it doesn't evolve overnight. *Forrest Gump* was ten years in the making. Arthur Schnitzler's 1926 novella, *Rhapsody, a Dream Novel,* was turned into the 1999 Stanley Kubrick film, *Eyes Wide Shut.* Patricia Highsmith's haunting novel *The Talented Mr. Ripley,* first published in 1955, also took until 1999 to be transformed to the screen, by Academy Award–winning director Anthony Minghella. It all takes time, dedication, and a lot of money.

If approximately 50,000 new books are published in America each year (albeit many of them textbooks and children's books) and the major Hollywood studios and independents make 200 to 300 films a year, then some 49,700 new titles are *not* soon going to be a major motion picture.

Most film purchases revolve around fiction bestsellers and brand-name authors. Many books are optioned and bought for the screen, but few get to the development stage. They fail to get "packaged" with the right director, stars, screenwriter, and financial backing, and they languish on the producer's or purchaser's dusty shelves of movies-in-waiting. In recent years, these have included such bestsellers as *The Liars' Club, Snow in August,* and *The Gold Coast.*

The reasons for the usually long transformation from book to film are the exorbitant costs involved and the star ingredients that make up the package. The average studio film now costs around fifty million dollars; independents cost somewhat less. Much of the cost is "above the line"—payment commitments to the stars, the producer, director, and screenwriter, and the purchase price of the book or intellectual property on which the film is based.

If your stars were Tom Hanks and Julia Roberts and your director was Martin Scorsese, your above-the-line costs could approach fifty million before a reel was shot. It is not necessarily the cost of making the movie that balloons the budget (*Titanic* and special-effects films are the exceptions); it is the signing of the talent.

The Blair Witch Project, a sleeper film that was financed by young people on a shoestring and ended up captivating the American public while grossing over a hundred million dollars, is the very rare exception.

Bestsellers, commercial thrillers, and human dramas are the kinds of books bought for eventual filming. Occasionally, true-life stories like *A Civil Action, The Perfect Storm,* and *Angela's Ashes* are made into movies. Older novels are constantly being optioned as potential films but are greatly dependent on that "package" materializing. If bankable filmmakers like Stephen Spielberg announce their next film idea— *Amistad* or *Memoirs of a Geisha*—it usually gets made. *Uber* agent Michael Ovitz was a Hollywood deal maker who controlled a lot of packages. He provided the stars and the director and made projects bankable endeavors for the studios to finance. His famous lament, apocryphal or not, was "Why are my clients getting ninety percent of my income?"

Many bestselling authors, like Danielle Steel, Judith Krantz, and Jackie Collins, prefer that their novels be converted into longer-form miniseries or "two-nighters" for television rather than feature films. Others are hesitant about licensing their works to the screen. Sue Grafton has been reluctant to turn her *A Is for Alibi*—and on through the rest of the alphabet— series into movies, probably for the obvious reason. If film number one fails at the box office, as it did with Sara Paretsky's V. I. Warshawski detective series novels, then there is no likelihood of a sequel, or in this bestselling case—an entire alphabet of sequels.

After my tenure as president of Pinnacle Books, I acquired the film rights to our extraordinarily successful *Destroyer* series, authored by Warren Murphy and

Dick Sapir. The James Bondian satirical quality of this bestselling saga was ideally adaptable to the screen. Additionally, it was a seventy-volume established series that had sold millions of copies around the world. I sincerely believed that not only could it be a commercially viable film, but it could lead to a franchise, à la James Bond. In my dreams I was rich, living off accumulated royalties from an aggregate of up to seventy films, sequels, remakes, spin-offs. What a financial coup for me and for the deserving authors.

But I forgot about the "first movie syndrome," the Sue Grafton movie hesitation rule. There were ominous signs at the outset. I brought the project to Dick Clark and his TV production company for their first foray into feature films. I couldn't have found a finer gentleman and a finer company. That was the good news. They had to associate with a major studio for financing and distribution. Orion Pictures entered as our film partner. They would virtually control the decision making and the budget because they were paying.

Their first decision was to change the title of this popular worldwide series with its millions of devotees. *The Destroyer* became *Remo Williams* (the protagonist's name), and then they added the ill-fated subtitle

The Adventure Begins. Next, although the authors wrote in a unique whimsical style, and Warren had previously written the screenplay for Clint Eastwood's *The Eiger Sanction,* Orion chose its own screenwriter to adapt *The Destroyer*—I mean *Remo,* not an unusual Hollywood move. They then cast no major stars for the dual leads, although Joel Grey and Fred Ward were creditable actors, if not box-office names.

The movie that ultimately came to the screen wasn't bad. But it wasn't great. It had the wrong title and handle, and it didn't generate big dollars at the turnstiles. It was quickly relegated to video, where it has performed enduringly well over the years. But it did not segue into two to seventy sequels—and I didn't retire after my baptism as a movie producer. It was also my first participation in "backend" money, the money that principals (not those like Julia Roberts and Mel Gibson who get *gross* dollars off the top) receive *after* a film earns out. Backend money is *net* profits—after everything is deducted, including all necessary hairdressers, limos, and craft services—and rarely materializes in the form of large checks. In the filmic life of *Remo Williams,* there were *no* checks.

Although the bestseller, the latest thriller, and the older novel are often acquired for film, most movies evolve from ideas, concepts, or original screenplays. Once you have protected your idea and are ready to offer it to the movies, the real drama begins.

To whom do you submit? What do you do initially? You start to network—by dining at the right watering holes and making the appropriate film contacts. It may be somebody's cousin, someone's entertainment attorney, some friend's sister's relative at a studio or Ovitz-type agency. You need to be filmically connected. The connection leads up the pecking ladder from an agent to a producer to a production company to a money person or financier to a studio or movie distributor. You need to be "greenlighted" along the way (everybody saying yes to your film idea until it is funded and the movie is made).

So you register it, and you lunch at Spago's, and your uncle's niece reads for Miramax, and you connect. If you can snare a superagent or agency—the big guys are William Morris, CAA, ICM, the new Mike Ovitz shop, and United Talent or Renaissance—it's a start up that ladder. Then, hopefully, a production company steps in and loves your idea/concept/story. They may be New Line, Castle Rock, Gaylord Entertainment— but they still need the mega studio to finance and distribute. There are not many of those. They are 20th

Century-Fox, Warner Bros., Universal, Disney/Miramax, Paramount, Sony/Columbia, and sometimes MGM/ United Artists, and they ultimately pay the $50 million speculative investment.

If you're not lunching or living in Hollywood, as most creators are not, you've got to find that connecting agent or attorney who can submit and solicit for you. Perhaps you know an author who has previously sold to the movies. Or, as an opportunistic gamble—if you've got absolutely the hottest new film concept or property in town—you write to Stephen Spielberg at Dreamworks/Universal Studios—or to his wife, Kate Capshaw, or his partners, Jeffrey Katzenberg or David Geffin, at the same address. Use your ingenuity, use your contacts. Get your script or treatment to someone who can make *your* movie.

Your entertainment attorney, agent, or representative signs a contract for you, and you may or may not receive advance monies, be greenlighted, be asked to write the screenplay (probably not), and be apprised of a film schedule (probably not). You will most likely wait—and hope to see your name on the big screen. "They" have to develop (write the treatment, hire a scriptwriter, sign on stars and a director, create a budget, find a location, hire a staff) and then shoot a movie. It will happen—now, in your lifetime, or post-humously—or it won't. Such are the mercurial ways and whims of Hollywood.

The deal you will receive is dependent on numerous factors and variables. Bestselling books will be bought early and often—generally in the manuscript or galley stage. *The Horse Whisperer,* in its early forms, was faxed from England and acquired by Robert Redford and Disney after only a few chapters crossed the ocean. Stephen King's serial novel, *The Green Mile,* was bought and developed immediately for film production. Some fifty King bestsellers, including novels, novellas, and short stories, have been filmed in recent decades, ranging in genre from *The Shawshank Redemption* to *Carrie* to *Stand by Me. The Cider House Rules,* John Irving's celebrated novel, was acquired prior to best-sellerdom and languished at the studio development level for a while until they found an acceptable person to write the screenplay—John Irving, who ultimately won an Academy Award for "Best Screenplay Adaptation." Well-plotted published books are next in priority, followed by unpublished or not-yet-published books, followed by treatments and outlines and synopses. The less material that is presented for a full-length feature film, the greater the likelihood that someone has to write an entire script and some director has to envision what that movie will be. They are unlikely to utilize *you,* the author or creator, in any other capacity than as a consultant. You will ultimately be accorded screen credit as author of the property.

Up-front deals and packages vary depending on the immediacy of a project, the availability of committed stars, and the studio or production company execs who are in power at the time. The movie moguls are a transient group, subject to parent company and stockholder mandates to make money and to produce the next *Star Wars* or *Austin Powers.* When "their" money doesn't realize a handsome return on investment or, God forbid, any return on investment, "they" get itchy and spin the musical chairs to find another film psychic. Of course, the stark reality, as we've stated previously, is that nobody knows what next year's box office hits are going to be.

Your idea, concept, full treatment, screenplay, or manuscript might warrant an outright buy or an option step deal against future payments. A typical arrangement might be $30,000 down for a one-year option against a $300,000 purchase price, payable one-half on acquisition and one-half on start of "principal photography" (the actual start of filming). There will be a clause that extends the option beyond a year, for more money, once the initial year option expires. If your film project revolves around a recurring protagonist (James Bond or Austin Powers) and/or a continuity series or sequels (*The Destroyer*), the acquiring company or producer will inevitably tie up all film and live media rights in perpetuity.

Additionally, all of this advance money will be applied against a share of net profits, or backend participation, usually in the author range of 2.5 to 5 points (2.5 to 5 percent of net). You may—sometimes, as needed—get more dollars as consultant on the film, which would mean you might have to be on the set every day, hanging around people like Sharon Stone or Kevin Costner. But you get to keep the up-front money regardless of profits.

Recently, super bestselling author Michael Crichton, author of *Jurassic Park* and *Disclosure*, effected an unprecedented arrangement with Paramount Pictures. He will be the first author to receive a percentage of box-office profits, or front-end monies, for the film version of his new novel, *Timeline*. This unique deal will be in lieu of large advance monies paid outright for a future bestseller.

Your Hollywood agent (rarely can you do it yourself) will make you the best deal possible. With luck your project will be embraced by bankable stars and a creditable director, and the movie will get made. Or it will sit, waiting for a catalyst to put it into development. To run through the process again, in more detail: Development is the long, sometimes arduous, process of preparing a property for filming. First comes the treatment, then the first-draft screenplay, then rewrites and a polish or two. The ultimate and acceptable script must be approved by a committee of mavens—the director, the star names above the credits, the producer, the suits or the money people, the head honcho at the studio level, and perhaps the CEO of the parent company.

After script approval, the budget is created—*above the line* (the talent) and *below the line* (the cost of making the movie)—and it quickly gets into the millions. It is a tight, rigid budget that will inevitably increase in time. Somehow it never gets reduced, particularly if weather, problems on the set, or "acts of God" delay or postpone filming.

Then your movie starts to sign up the cast and everybody else needed to make the film. A shooting schedule is set. Principal photography will commence on a given date. The dark side of this Hollywood scenario is that most of the above plans do not materialize and you are trapped in "development hell" indefinitely. At worst, this may lead to turnaround: your project is dropped from the studio slate; you get to keep the option money to date; and you don't get to meet Julia or Demi. Before you cry in your single malt, however, remember that films like *Star Wars* and *Forrest Gump* were once in turnaround. Keep this in mind: if your movie makes it to the big screen, a lot of time will have passed by.

Where are the very beginnings of this journey to a major or even a minor motion picture? Learn the craft. Learn the business. Read the books, particularly the bibles on screenwriting, written by recognized gurus like Syd Field, Robert McKee, Linda Seger, and a few others. Take some courses on screenwriting—at the University of California at Los Angeles (UCLA), the University of Southern California (USC), or New York University (NYU), Northwestern, or at any of the extension programs listed in your region. Many adult and community college programs now feature a primary course on Introduction to Film, or How to Write a Script. Syd Field and other recognized screenwriting teachers have on-line workshops as well. Also, see a lot of movies, and read the scripts of major films. They are often published in book format. And stay clued in by reading *Variety* and the *Hollywood Reporter*.

A typical film treatment might titillate your prospective buyer if it read along these lines:

Somewhere between Euphoria and Sacramento lies the happy hamlet of Sand City, California. Incorporated in 1936, it would surely have served as President Alf Landon's Western White House. Nestled between three Denny's, two Arby's, and a Domino's Pizza, Sand City boasts a college, appropriately named Sand City State; a library; a fine-arts center; and a senior citizens' home.

One afternoon during the annual Alums vs. Residents' softball game, the Sand City Memorial Senior Citizens' Home burns to the ground. Luckily, no one is killed or injured in the fire, and life goes on uninterrupted in Sand City. Except the senior citizens need a place to live.

In a dramatic court petition, with national media reverberations, a judge awards the seniors—now the Sand City Seniors—a house on the corner of Sand City State College whose lease will be expiring. Everything will work out—except for one thing. The present tenants—Sigma Upsilon Delta Fraternity, the SUDS house on campus—have no intention of leaving. A court order is granted to the senior citizens . . . but a writ of *no evictus corpus* is also handed down. There is only one viable solution. The Sand City Seniors and the SUDS brothers will all live together in the fraternity house.

It is probably essential that you learn the appropriate format for writing a screenplay. Usually one page of dialogue or action fills a minute on the screen, so a 115-page script translates to about a 115-minute movie. Film scripts are more controlled and tighter than novels. They are all dialogue and directions. There is no room for narrative or lengthy description. The dialogue and what the actor does with the dialogue (the nuances, the gestures) are the integral ingredients. Movies are also the most visual of media, and the segue from a literary bestseller like *The English Patient* by Michael Ondaatje to the magnificent film directed by Anthony Minghella is the result of writing on the page being translated visually.

Most of the instructive screenwriting books show you the format of a screenplay. It is a different kind of writing, restricted in length. You've got two hours or less to tell and show a movie, the exceptions being epics like *Gone with the Wind, Dr. Zhivago, Dances with Wolves, Titanic.* You've got to portray characters and characterizations. The title characters in *Thelma and Louise* were wonderfully portrayed by Susan Sarandon and Geena Davis because the screenplay (a first) by Callie Kouri gave them life and feeling and panache. It gave them powerful, evocative roles. As an old cliché goes, "If it ain't on the page, it ain't on the stage."

Your screenplay may be based on another medium— *your* novel or play or someone else's—or it may extend from an idea or treatment you created. The premise of *Saving Private Ryan* evolved from a true-life story about the last surviving son of a family whose other sons were all killed in a world war and the quest to get *him* out of combat alive. The simple thesis of *You've Got Mail* is that two people who connect as e-mail correspondents ultimately meet and fall in love via the Internet. Ideas flow from our own lives and personal experiences, from true-life events, and from deep within our imagination.

Selling to the movies is a more difficult task. It is about timing and luck and finding the "greenlighter" who has the power and influence to make your movie a reality. *Mask,* a first film effort by Anna Hamilton Phelan, was written in Syd Field's screenwriting class, and the right film connections were made. Kevin Costner fell in love with the baseball novel *For Love of the Game* and was obsessed about making the film. Producer Wendy Finerman believed in *Forrest Gump* from the outset and persevered through many a rejection to make one of the more memorable commercial films of our era.

You've got to get your screen project, when ready, to somebody bankable—star, producer, director, packaging agent, super deal honcho, or the movie production company that will pay for it all. And you can't get discouraged. Rejections and long waits are part of the process. You almost have to play amateur casting director. If your film idea is a perfect vehicle for Meg Ryan, you have to get it to her—somehow, some way—via her agent, friends of hers, a publicist, or just by writing to her—in Hollywood, or at her ranch near Bozeman, Montana. You have to be pleasantly aggressive, and you have to keep your project in play. The lesson evoked is the story of the old man who prays to God every night, "Please dear God, just let me win the lottery before I die." Finally God appears before him and says, "Sidney, I'm willing to meet you halfway. *Buy a ticket.*" In Hollywood, you have to buy a ticket and keep your script out there so somebody can read it and hopefully buy it.

In recent years, literary classics from a century or more ago, now in the public domain, have been discovered for the screen. Shakespeare, Henry James, and

Jane Austen are dramatic examples, but some obscure titles have also been adapted for film. Very advantageously, there is no purchase price to be paid, no royalties, no backend. Just give credit where it is due, to authors like Homer and Cervantes. Sometimes the original work gets creatively distorted or bastardized, as Shakespeare's *Richard III* metamorphosed into a dark Nazi-era movie version, and Jane Austen's *Emma* segued into the teen teaser *Clueless*. If you base your screenplay on a book in the public domain, you can alter it as you wish. It could be your mix of *Don Quixote* and *Travels with Charley* or David and Goliath and *Rocky*.

In your quest for a motion picture sale, remember to envision what else your film could be. Is there likelihood of a book emanating from the film? a CD-ROM or electronic game? merchandising spin-offs? Think about the exploitational potential. In this age of hype and hustle, it is not far-fetched to project *Romeo and Juliet* being sold as a designer brand at Victoria's Secret or Dante's *Inferno* being an underground interactive game. Envision it; you can plan it from the outset if you are clever and opportunistic and know your media marketplace.

Years ago, when I spoke to a grade school class about

John Steinbeck's literary masterpiece *Of Mice and Men* and the original classic film it became, one investigative young mind had a revelation. "I'll bet that guy Steinbeck saw the movie and then wrote a book about it." Today, he might have.

Television is many things to many people—particularly to the people in the business. Hundreds of channels now feature network and cable versions of sitcoms, reality shows, dramas, dramadies (a mix of both), miniseries, talk shows, news shows, live events, sports, history, infomercials, home shopping, MOWs (movies of the week), even a Weather Channel. There is something for everyone, and "surfin' the tube" is an American pastime. TV is also a medium that reaches millions of viewers instantly. Twenty million people may watch *60 Minutes,* or *Who Wants To Be a Millionaire,* or *The Practice* each time the programs air. Over a hundred million may be the audience for an event like the Academy Awards or the Super Bowl or for an international tragedy like the startling deaths of Princess Diana and John F. Kennedy Jr. Television provides instant coverage, instant entertainment, and it reaches you right in your own home.

Creating for television requires a road map, a certain amount of chicanery, cleverness, and the right contacts at the propitious time. It is such a transient, erratic medium because there are no guarantees when it comes to what gets on the air and what stays on the air. Whereas most books acquired by a publishing house ultimately get published, most TV pilots or concepts in development don't get shown on the tube and are never seen or heard from again. And yet some shows endure over six or seven or more years, and their eventual cancellations are lamented by millions of devotees. See under *Mash, Cheers, Seinfeld,* et al. *Your* created show or TV program may be unique, imaginative, and commercial, but it may never get on the air. Such are the mercurial ways and whims of television and its orchestrators—the producers and the advertisers.

The term *high concept* describes those commercial and easily describable TV shows and ideas that are immediately recognizable to everybody. They are concepts that sound like success formulas that have worked in the past. Their *TV Guide* blurbs would read "*Golden Girls* set in Las Vegas," "a Black or Hispanic *Friends*," "*Third Rock from the Sun* with *Mash*." A high concept premise for nonentertainment programming would be combining eBay auctions with Home Shopping. The opposite of high concept isn't low concept but rather ideas that are somewhat groundbreaking and innovative and difficult to pigeonhole by TV execs.

It's a competitive business, and few ideas emerge

for mass television viewing. But the pessimistic warnings do have a flip side—a sanguine outlook for creators—because there are more programming opportunities than ever before. Cable has opened up new vistas, including niche channels that focus on special subjects like history, science, and sports. There is now an unlimited market for fresh, imaginative ideas that can be original or derived from books and other media properties. Bestselling books and commercial novels in the thriller, romance, and horror genres are often bought and converted into one- to three-night movies of the week or miniseries. *Lonesome Dove* was an award-winning example. So was *Barbarians at the Gate*. The heartwarming bestseller *Tuesdays with Morrie* evolved into a memorable television drama starring Jack Lemmon as Morrie. Like feature films, notable books are bought early and assigned to a scriptwriter. The time requirements for television are approximately twenty-two out of every thirty minutes for the program or movie, and eight minutes for commercials. A script for a two-hour TV movie would run close to ninety minutes.

If your creative idea is oriented to television, and it is original, derivative, or formulaic, you have to know exactly *where* to place it. That is a challenge. How do you know that your original concept hasn't been thought of before and is being developed for television as you write? You don't. You have to protect (register) it as best you can, get it to the right prospective buyer, and hope it is so topically unique and commercial that it gets on the air before the competitors and imitators. Timing, once again, is essential.

Assuming you know what you've written, you should be familiar with that television form (e.g., sitcom, MOW, drama) and who is producing those particular shows and formats. The biggest names—like David Kelley (*Ally McBeal, The Practice*) and Aaron Spelling (*Melrose Place* and myriad others)—are bankable in every TV genre. Others, like Dick Clark Productions, are known for game and award shows or annual event shows like *The Golden Globes*. Suzanne DePasse, of *Lonesome Dove,* creates in the long form of miniseries. Merv Griffin Productions produces *Jeopardy* and *Wheel of Fortune*. The listings of all current shows and productions and their creators can be found in the movie/TV trade publications (*Premiere* magazine, *Movieline,* the *Hollywood Reporter, Variety, Ross Reports, TV Guide,* and your local newspaper) and in *Written By*—the magazine of the Writers Guild of America. Additionally, there is an excellent book on the mechanics of television writing—*A Friend in the Business,* by Robert Masello.

You should familiarize yourself with these shows and watch them fairly regularly if you want to write or create for them. They are all listed weekly in *TV Guide* and span the major networks and cable channels. Of course, what may emerge on the air next year may have little relation to this year's offerings, although formulas tend to repeat themselves with exaggerated regularity. Then there are the spin-offs and segues and character extensions. The most significantly successful of these evolved from *The Mary Tyler Moore Show*, which spawned *Rhoda*, *Phyllis*, and *Lou Grant*. *Cheers* introduced *Frazier*. *NYPD Blue* was naturally hatched from *LA Law*. And on and on. In this case, familiarity breeds *content*, more and more familiar content.

The innovative concept—something completely new—like *Third Rock from the Sun* or *Judging Amy*— may or may not work, depending on the public's acceptance and the initial ratings. When the advertisers are happy, so are the networks, and the show, or shows, will go on.

Another type of television format is the "one-shot"— an event show or anniversary tie-in or special hyped subject. Revealing the contents of Al Capone's vault or reprising the life of Lady Di are prototypical examples. So was my first foray into television—the creation and production of *The Elvis Files* and then *The Marilyn Files*.

Beyond the one-shot, there is also an enduring TV market for nonfiction subjects and serial fiction, much of this derived from books. The now-immortalized *Chicken Soup for the Soul* industry has become a weekly television series on Pax Net, the family cable network; the *Random Acts of Kindness* series is coming to TV; *Waldo* evolved as a children's show; and Robert Parker's novels segued into an ongoing series, *Spencer,* featuring the books' protagonist. When I was president of Pinnacle Books, we published Geraldine Saunders's reminiscences of her years as hostess of *The Love Boat.* We did not envision then that a few years later this delightful memoir would become one of the most beloved and commercial weekly series of all time.

We also published classic series like *Tarzan* and *Hornblower,* which have enjoyed numerous television lives over the decades. When a series hits, not only can it run for years but it achieves lucrative value as a vehicle for unlimited rerun syndication throughout the world. Successful examples include original iconic sitcoms like *I Love Lucy* and *The Mary Tyler Moore Show.* Programs like *Jeopardy* and *Wheel of Fortune* have been internationally syndicated as well.

The game show has recently been revitalized. In the 1950s legendary TV game shows like *The $64,000 Question, Twenty-One,* and *What's My Line?* ruled the airways, but quiz show scandals ended the reign of the big giveaway shows. In the new millennium, the form has been recycled as *Who Wants to Be a Millionaire*, hosted by Regis Philbin.

The "strip show"—one that airs every weekday night—is a profitable venture for producer, network, and creator/writers. Its subject matter necessarily features themes that can be repeated in format five nights a week. A&E's *Biography Series* aptly illustrates this concept—a similar format but focusing on a different person each show. Venerable programs like *60 Minutes*, *20/20*, and *Dateline* started out as one-nighters but soon blossomed into syndicated shows that appear on multiple nights. The rationale had to do with their recognition factor in appealing to receptive audiences and with being relatively cheap to produce.

It is unlikely that you will write segments for *60 Minutes*, ongoing plots for soap operas like *The Young and The Restless*, or weekly scripts for *E.R.* They have their built-in writers (a group of them) who work exclusively on these shows and are paid well. Your spec script for *The Practice* or *Everybody Loves Raymond* would have trouble ending up on the air, but it could be valuable in serving as a good sample of your work. It could aid and advance your efforts the next time out.

An area for potential breakthroughs in television is

the lucrative world of selling via the Home Shopping or QVC Networks or infomercials. The criterion for selection is a configuration of books and/ or videos, audios, posters, collectibles, etc. that can generate sales of at least $250,000 an hour. The only way to accomplish this is to package multimedia products that feature approximately a $25 book, a $25 tape, and related merchandise.

When I conceived and published *The Movie Script Library* in association with *Premiere* magazine, we created a package that we launched on the QVC Network. This collectible series of original scripts and lobby cards of the celebrated movies of our lives featured *Gone with the Wind, The Wizard of Oz, It's a Wonderful Life,* and numerous other classic films. We enhanced the *Star Wars* package by having star Mark Hamill sign individual scripts to create a $100 collectible instead of a $20 retail book. Sold with the script was a *Star Wars* video and a poster. The *Star Trek* scripts were autographed by Leonard Nimoy in a similar multimedia offering. The venture was enormously successful and was replicated several times. It was an ideal formula for home shopping solicitations, one of few that were book-based.

The infomercial—an entertaining, informative tele-

vision show whose format is used to sell a product—
has been an integral part of late-night TV for some
time now. The show usually runs about an hour, sometimes a half hour, and subtly but with hard-sell over-
tones *info*rms you about a subject, then hard-sells it to
you—the com*mercial*. It has been an effective vehicle
for selling products from steak knives to secrets of
training your dog to the latest gimmick for dying rich.
The approach is based on hooking you in with the fascinating subject matter. You are tempted to watch
these entertaining and informative shows, and even
more tempted to buy. Sometimes they are based on a
book or mass media concept, but more often they are
selling a product that you didn't know you coveted or
needed but suddenly feel compelled to buy. The infomercial titillates you and motivates your spontaneous
purchase. Suddenly you own the latest juice squeezer,
or pills to make you younger. You have been "info-
mercialized."

For you—the neophyte—to break into this potentially lucrative world, you have to study the formulas
and format, have a product or range of products that
will motivate purchase, and be able to buy the time
that will justify your investment. Your product may
evolve from a book or video or other media concept,

but it must fulfill the sales criteria and motivate people to buy. Remember, why do we need this product, and why do we need it at this time?

As with the other mass media, it is essential that you study the medium and all of its variables. The range and scope of potential TV markets extend from sitcoms, dramas, and soaps to nonfiction, informative, and educational subjects. Television can cover every imaginable subject and present it in different formats—long or short form—over one night or weeks and months.

You must be familiar with the type of show for which you are creating and writing. Each show is different in format and content. Once you know your targeted TV market, you can create your original idea in the appropriate format for that show or type of program. If your concept is unique and has not been tried before, you will have to find a buyer and begin your sales solicitations. That is the difficult challenge. If your project is totally innovative, you will necessarily have to educate the marketplace as well as sell to it. Your facilitator may be an agent, an attorney, a contact in the television industry, or you may work alone, a more difficult undertaking.

After you have registered your idea or concept and protected it as best you can, you will have to show it around. Most of the TV markets and buyers are based on the West Coast, although there are development and production entities in New York and in Canada. Once you know to whom you want to submit your idea, you have to reach that market via the most direct and reliable contact possible. You have to find and ask people with prior TV experience to provide you with key contact names, or research the television trade publication for the appropriate producer in your genre of endeavor. Your registered treatment is your best sample or calling card, and the opening pitch that should titillate the prospective TV buyer might be similar to the following:

THE HUNTED

It is the present. We are in a small town, Spark, Florida, known for its prison and "old Sparky," the electric chair that slowly fried rather than quickly killed its victims.

Spark is also where the youth hunts take place every year. It is a town filled with good, religious people who ritualistically take their fine young sons out to hunt, to prey on, to kill the unforeseeing deer that are systematically herded together so that each boy will be assured a good clean shot.

"We'll kill anything that moves," said one eight-year-old, proudly displaying his deer.

The parents (fathers) see the hunt as a rite of passage into manhood. There is a frenzied, almost insane competition among the youngsters to see who can make a kill first and kill the biggest buck.

The Florida Fresh Water Fish and Game Commission quietly sanctions these hunts. They don't get in the way of the zealots who run the hunt.

But some people do—some like Marni Walters, the school psychologist, and Richard Cowan, the senator's aide. They are about to descend into a world they know nothing about—the world of the hunt—the world where the sport of blood is seen as a right—solemn and sacred.

Your hope and fantasy are that someone will buy it as soon as possible and it won't be hanging around out there in TV oblivion.

If you are fortunate enough to be able to submit to a major TV production company, working producer, or credible buyer and your project is acquired for television development (usually on an option or step deal basis), then you wait through the interminable period of development. There are myriad steps in this process, from writing treatments and spec scripts and planning the essential ingredients of the TV show or concept, to actual development for airing. If you get to this stage and a network (ABC, CBS, NBC, Warner, Paramount, or Fox, cable outlets like HBO and Showtime, or specialty channels like Lifetime, A&E, USA, or others) buys your idea, you are very close to the reality of getting on the air. Few shows do.

I don't mean to project a pessimistic scenario, but the odds for outright hits are similar to those for blockbuster movies and bestselling books. Only a handful break through. But successes can be achieved in the television medium by creating and selling for niche as well as mainstream markets. There are few *Mash* series or *Love Boats*, few *Jeopardy* game shows, limited *Nightline* programs, but there are many new sitcoms, and there is much innovative programming each year. And there are constant new outlets and markets for development and solicitation. You've got to watch and study the mercurial marketplace. You've also got to view all the shows for which you hope to create and sell.

If you get to the deal stage, you will need an agent or attorney to negotiate for you. Television contracts are traditionally intricate and often obscure, featuring terminology not familiar to the neophyte. The essential deal ingredients will include all the contingency situations that may evolve, from development to creating a pilot to ultimate production. You will invariably receive a percentage of every show aired plus residuals in perpetuity if a series or reruns, syndication, or foreign sales materialize.

Finally, no one said you couldn't initiate a new form. You can create a new concept, a new format for television viewing. Unique series like *Survivor, The Sopranos,* and *Sex in the City* and reality-based news programs like *48 Hours* and *20/20* were groundbreaking formats in the television medium. So was *Sesame Street* in its genre. There may be an interminable period from gestation of an idea to its ultimate appearance on the television screen, or it may not eventuate at all. Such are the long and realistic odds. However, any success in the TV medium can be extraordinarily lucrative because of the sheer numbers. Book bestsellers and film box-office bonanzas can reach mass audiences, but they can't reach twenty to thirty million people (and more) in a single viewing. The magnitude of the television audience is such that the entire world can watch an event unfold.

Learn the medium, study the various types of content and formats and the marketability of new ideas for both network and cable solicitation. Read the industry publications and *TV Guide* on a regular basis, and follow the emerging trends and shifts in programming.

Also, stay particularly attuned to the synergistic opportunities to exploit your idea in another medium.
Projects derived from books and movies have been developed as TV series and specials. Recent examples already noted include *Buffy the Vampire Slayer, Spencer,
Goodnight Moon,* and *Tuesdays with Morrie.*

Your original television concept may be merchandisable in another medium or may have exploitable
spin-off possibilities. If twenty million people have seen
a TV show, there will be a receptive market for almost
any derivative product. The prospects for television
global expansion and its Internet linkups are unlimited.
Hundreds of channels on every imaginable subject will
be plugged into our homes. The dissemination of news,
entertainment, and information will continue to be instant and constant. We will be junkies for the latest,
greatest, fastest, and trendiest in media messaging. The
marketing of media products could revolve in a contin-
uous and perpetual cycle. Read the bestselling book
based on the hit TV program, which evolved from the
blockbuster movie, which was created from the book.
For further information, check your *TV Guide* or the
Web site of this media product. Or better yet, look it
all up on your own Web site.

The video revolution of about a decade ago turned out to be a passing media phenomenon. It was upstaged and supplanted by CD-ROMs and then by the ultimate revolution and revelation of the Internet. When videos became the new hot medium in the 1980s, every media product that was book- or film-based "went straight to video." As paperbacks had become the second publication life of hardcover books, home videos became the secondary market for movies. Within six months to a year, all released films (and some never released theatrically) ended up as videos. The "sell-through" videos—usually the very popular movies—were priced in the $19.95 range or sometimes as low as $12.95 for mass consumption. "They" wanted you to buy *Titanic* and *Saving Private Ryan* and *The Lion King*. Video releases of movies are now available in DVD format. Other films were priced for rental, their retail prices being prohibitive for purchase. Most videos were being sold at the chain video stores like Blockbuster and Music Plus and at bookstores; the mass popular movies were ultimately being made available at supermarket checkout counters.

Additionally, all nonfiction subjects, most derived from bestselling books, became ideal content for video reproduction. How to make money, exercise, and dance of every variety; cooking, sports, parenting, and hobbies—all became video subjects. The bestsellers in the field were led by the workout videos, dominated by celebrity names like Jane Fonda, Kathy Smith, and Kathy Ireland. Other popular nonfiction video subjects revolved around home repair and gardening. How-to and children's videos also became instantly popular and functional. Harvey Penick's bestselling books on golf wisdom became *Harvey Penick's Little Green Video*. The antithesis was the popular video *Leslie Nielsen's Bad Golf My Way*. The admired Suze Orman titles and seminars were transformed into her *9 Steps to Financial Freedom* video. Videos soon emerged on fitness subjects like Tai Chi and yoga, not to mention titles like *Abs of Steel*, and *Buns of Steel*. New Age topics proliferated in video format, as well as millennial historical retrospectives of our past century and past lives. An original concept in one of the formula bestselling categories could also be commercially viable. The market was unlimited because everyone was purchasing videos for home use.

Sometimes videos became the aftermarket for popular TV series or shows, like our *Elvis* and *Marilyn Files* specials. Video budgets for book subjects ranged from $25,000 to $150,000, depending upon the above-the-line costs (the fees paid to the host narrator and to any stars who appeared in the video). When I coproduced Jan Stephenson's golf video and Pete Rose's motivational tape, the major costs were for the stars themselves.

In planning to market your concept or project for a video, you must prepare a sample—which would necessarily include your selling title and blurb (similar to a book presentation), outline of subject matter and continuity of the video, and some filmed footage (at least ten minutes of actual time). Remember that your video will be viewed, not read, and your visual presentation is crucial to effecting a sale. Your blurb or tag line should evoke a viewer response. For the Pete Rose sports tape, we featured the blurb "A motivating program to inspire anyone who strives toward success." Of course, that motivating line might have been used on numerous packages of inspirational videos.

Format is a key ingredient in planning a video. Your video, like a movie, will be directed as well as written. The probable length—from sixty to ninety minutes—must be calculated, and decisions about who is on camera and how long are also important. You do not want a video of just "talking heads," which would em-

ulate a lecture format. You must calibrate video continuity, message, and the actors' roles and participation.
Background music may also be needed.

When your video sample is ready, you may submit
via your media agent, representative, or attorney. If you
are soliciting cold—and on speculation—find out which
video companies or producers specialize in your field.
Go to your local video store or large chain bookstore
(Borders, Barnes & Noble) and examine the videos on
specific subjects to ascertain the contact names of
their respective producers and production companies.
Additionally, you can purchase trade publications like
Ross Reports, Video Watchdog, and *Widescreen Review* for further video industry information. Send them
a query letter (similar to the book proposal query in
chapter 5) only oriented to the visual video market and
ask if they would like to see and evaluate your sample.
If you have created a unique and commercial video
concept, you will most likely receive a positive response.

The deal for the author or creator of a videotape
usually includes an advance against a royalty percentage, similar to a book publication contract. The earn-
ing potential (with Kathy Smith–type rare exceptions)
is not huge, but it is often steady. The video revolution
was short-lived, but it stills thrives, in lesser propor-

tions, as a source of information and entertainment and a media alternative to books, CD-ROMs, DVDs, and audios.

One of the more phenomenal breakthrough areas in the media world over the past decade has been the emergence of the spoken audiotape—on cassette or CD. No one imagined that people would listen to a bestseller being read or to financial or estate planning advice transmitted to them on their car stereos while driving home from work. It was not an innovative electronic medium. But the believers proved the experts wrong. Led by companies like Audio Renaissance, Dove, Books on Tape, Brilliance, and major book publishers like Simon & Schuster, Bantam, HarperCollins, Random House, and Penguin, the audiotape transformed bestselling fiction into auditory experiences with thespian-quality narrations performed by recognized actors and actresses—and occasionally even the author.

Every bestseller generated a companion audiotape—fiction and nonfiction. Subject categories that were ideally suited for audio included business and finance, how-to, inspiration and motivation, learning a craft or trade, staying slim and fit, and travel writing. The tapes were invariably full sets in the retail range of $50 or condensed versions (usually fiction) at approximately $14.95 to $19.95. If the tapes were derived from current published books, they were priced similarly to the book. Exceptions would include the unabridged *Hannibal* audio priced at $39.95.

With consumers now listening to books instead of reading them, books on tape became an alternative market for authors and creators of information. Motivational and financial gurus like Tony Robbins, Zig Ziglar, and Suze Orman were selling millions of tapes to disciples who wanted to *hear* their messages. Winning subject formulas like *The Psychology of Selling, How to Retire Rich,* and *Getting Past No* were being bought by companies and organizations as well as individuals. Multiple audio collections appeared of Gerard Nierenberg's *The Complete Negotiator,* the heartening *Don't Sweat the Small Stuff* homilies, and the Joseph Campbell *Myth* series. Even old radio shows starring Burns and Allen, Jack Benny, and Amos and Andy were back "on the air" in new audiocassette formats. Charles Kuralt's bestselling book and TV series *On the Road* became a series of bestselling audios. So did Ken Burns's celebrated *Civil War* series. Stephen Covey's heralded books on 7 *Habits*—for whatever—were launched on his own Covey audiotape imprint. You could now lose weight, assimilate stock market tips, or access your innermost secrets by popping in a cassette on the way home from the office.

A tape bestseller sells about one-tenth the numbers of the corresponding book bestseller, but it has become a predictably steady market with a loyal audience. As one TV media executive said to me recently, "In my frenetic schedule, I don't read books anymore. I listen to them." Again, we are experiencing the ultimate media extensions and possibilities. Read the book, see the movie, listen to the tape, buy the T-shirt . . . has become more the exploitable likelihood than the isolated media happening. Our information and entertainment are being transmitted to us via a growing range of media.

The audiotape is almost always published simultaneously with the book it is based on. The listening audience wants to hear it at the same time the book audience wants to read it. For general nonfiction subjects not tied to a book, the release of the audio is less dependent on seasonal or timely publication. The exceptions, as with books and videos, are when instant events are produced as audios, or sports tapes are released at the outset of a new season.

The audiotape is often a media adjunct to book publication, but many nonfiction subjects have proliferated as original versions on audio. Recent examples have included Princeton Review's *Word Smart* and *How to Study* from Highbridge Audio.

Smaller regional audiotape publishers have emerged,

including Brain Sync out of Santa Fe; Sounds True in Boulder, Colorado; the aforementioned Highbridge, which produces Garrison Keiller in St. Paul, Minnesota; and Hay House in Carlsbad, California.

If you are creating exclusively for the audio market, it is desirable, although not mandatory, to base your idea on a current published book. The more extended the media exploitation of an individual product or idea, the greater the response and recognition will be from the consumer. You can create your own niche—for both book and audio dissemination—by focusing on a nonfiction topic that fulfills a basic need. Everyone wants to look and feel better, live longer, be thin and healthy, and make a lot of money. Instead of just reading about it, they now have the viable alternative of listening to these informative messages.

If your subject matter is bought for audio publication, you will most likely receive a basic advance against a small but escalated royalty percentage of net sales. The advances are generally modest for original concepts, substantially and progressively higher for audios derived from published books or potential bestsellers. This prospect becomes dramatically heightened when an "event" book is issued—a new Patricia Cornwell, Stephen King, or Mary Higgins Clark or the latest Harry Potter. Sometimes several items are offered in a

collection, like three Nelson DeMille fictional bestsellers on one tape, John Updike's selection of *The Best
American Short Stories,* or Tolkien's classic *Lord of the
Rings* trilogy. If the initial book printing and sales are
projected at one million copies, then the likely first
audio run will be approximately 100,000 to 200,000
copies.

Bestsellers are often issued in multiple formats at
varying retail prices—the unabridged full text of the
novel as well as the abridged version. Esteemed author/
educator Jonathan Kozol recounts how he visited a
Texas bookstore and curiously found a greatly abridged
rendition of Melville's classic novel *Moby-Dick* on tape.
He inquired of the young book clerk, "Of course, you
have the full book of *Moby-Dick*?" "What for?" replied
the clueless clerk. "You can listen to the audio."

Ideally, your audio product should be tied to and
cross-merchandised with another medium based on
the same idea. Your audio or video proposal should
be associated with a simultaneous book proposal and
perhaps a TV or Internet concept. Publishers think
multimedia in these new millennium years. A commercially viable book premise, particularly in a nonfiction field, should translate into an audio or other
current media product. You should think multimedia
exploitation from the outset of your creative develop-

ment. It will enhance your media prospects for successful sales, and it will influence the media buyer's decision to acquire your product. The synergy of audio/book, audio/television is currently more of a cross-marketing likelihood than a chance media happening.

Additionally, the corporate tie-in has evolved as a promising commercial market. An existing tape, or one based on a topical book—abridged or unabridged—may be suitable for a corporate mailing to prospective clients or to employee or stockholder lists or for use as a premium to sell their products. An inspirational or how-to type of audiotape is often useful in motivating employees or sales staffs or appealing to potential buyers of corporate products.

The Suze Orman or Philip McGraw audio packages of financial tapes are invariably utilized by large companies, including many Fortune 500 corporate behemoths. The Spencer Johnson and Ken Blanchard books and corollary tapes—ranging from their mega bestseller *The One Minute Manager* to Johnson's current *Who Moved My Cheese?*—have all been used effectively by a myriad of diverse companies to stimulate sales and motivate employees. Numerous motivational videos have been especially created for corporations, using their own logo or imprint.

Many of the sales for motivational, how-to, salesmanship, and self-improvement audios have been bulk purchases by large and small companies. Synergistically, the audio sales tend to generate book and other peripheral sales of similar products in varied ancillary markets. A company might distill small portions of a bestseller for its own manufactured and created tape, or it might produce an original tape oriented to its specialized market. That innovative tape may evolve into a subsequent or related media product. Companies may also sponsor the creation of an original tape, and a custom-marketed audio may be created with the imprimatur of the sponsoring corporation.

When you are producing and creating an original idea, try to determine if your creation lends itself to audio or video reproduction. This will enhance your product appeal and increase your chances of book publication if initially submitted as a book proposal. Know the characteristics of and the content criteria and formulas of commercial audio- and videotapes. Watch and listen to audios and videos in your category or field.

Prepare an audio sampling of your proposed tape, using a strong narrative voice. Your audio treatment will be similar to your book proposal, featuring the salient and commercial contents and telling why there is a market need for this particular audio concept. What successful audiotape is your idea similar to? What are additional ancillary markets, beyond retail stores, for quantity purchases of your tape?

Additionally, your tape idea may have particular potential for corporate usage and premium tie-ins. Be alert to these opportunities and future markets. The successful and bestselling audios and videos today all have multimedia application and are part of a configuration of mass market products. Book and media bestsellers like *Tuesdays with Morrie, Don't Sweat the Small Stuff,* and *The Seat of the Soul* illustrate this current multimedia trend and phenomenon. In today's ever-changing new media world, the answer to the question "Did you read the book?" may be, "No, but I listened to it."

We saw the movie—and we read or listened to the book—but never did we anticipate that our generation or our children's generation would also be buying the lunch box, the place mats, the socks, and the matching hats. We could not imagine that the licensing blitz of a decade ago would evolve into merchandising mania. Every media brand name or recognizable product is now potentially merchandisable.

The *Star Wars* prequel realized several thousand individual licensing sales—to every manufactured product imaginable, from all forms of clothing apparel to games and toys (electronic or fuzzy) to cups and dishes to napkins and tissues. It was perhaps the most hyped and well-orchestrated merchandising campaign in licensing history. And almost everything labeled *Star Wars* sold. And almost every licenser made money, although they paid handsomely for the privilege. The Pokémon and Harry Potter crazes have generated similar licensing frenzy.

Once upon a time, we affectionately referred to the licensing of a logo or brand name as selling the "decal rights." Decals were reproductions of a design that could be steam-ironed onto a T-shirt or cap. You could affix familiar logos like Coca-Cola and Kellogg's Corn Flakes onto other licensed products. Then the sports leagues—the NBA and the NFL—began to license their logos, soon followed by the individual teams.

Then everybody was buying and wearing Oakland Raiders jackets and caps or Dallas Cowboys or Boston Celtics T-shirts and sweatshirts. Then the jerseys of sports legends like Michael Jordan (number 23) and John Elway (number 7) and female soccer stars like Mia Hamm became an integral part of every young boy's and girl's school wardrobe.

The movies followed soon after. *Star Wars* (the original), *E.T.*, *Jurassic Park*, *The Lion King*—all started to merchandise their identifiable names and signature imprints. There were jackets and hats, posters and calendars—brand-name tie-ins ad infinitum. Books became licensable, as evidenced by *Horse Whisperer* paraphernalia, *Bridges of Madison County* paper products, and *Eloise* and *Stuart Little* merchandising items. Almost every known media concept had licensing potential and opportunity. The Hollywood rationale was "If we're spending twenty million dollars on advertising and media saturation, we may as well merchandise the hell out of our product. We're buying our own word-of-mouth advertising."

When the movies worked at the box office, the merchandising sold as well. When *Titanic* and *Ninja Turtles* evoked fan adoration, mega licensing sales followed immediately. McDonald's and Burger King launched mass giveaways of everything Pokémon and *Toy Story*. When the book series *Goosebumps* and *The Baby-Sitters Club* became cult favorites of kids all across America, the merchandising blitz of ancillary products ensued. The makers of lunch boxes and sneakers and calendars all want the "decal rights" to successful media products. They generate substantial income *if* the initial media concept is successful.

Sometimes it is not—and the subsequent licensing also fails to elicit consumer response. When *Batman I and II* became *Batman* too many, the public stopped buying their licensing by-products. It was a case of media oversaturation. Inundated with the merchandise—the cars, the weaponry, the masks, the insignia, the coloring books—consumers inevitably reached the point of indifference. Batmania soon evaporated as a media franchise, and licensers began seeking the next cult or nostalgia franchise.

Similarly, the media merchandising of movie launches

like *Howard the Duck, The Avengers,* and *Godzilla* failed to generate significant or enduring product sales. Their licensing life was dependent on the film's success. When ticket sales didn't materialize for the film, it didn't work for the spin-off products. The consumer wants only the media winners—not the losers.

An unusual merchandising circumstance occurred in 1980 when President Jimmy Carter precipitously canceled U.S. participation in the Olympics scheduled to be hosted by Russia. An entrepreneurial friend of mine controlled the world licensing rights to the Olympic mascot—Misha the Bear. Transglobal deals had been negotiated for Misha apparel and toys and a myriad of licensing products. A potential merchandising bonanza had to be aborted as the United States withdrew its formal participation. Misha dolls were never unwrapped and soon became collector's items, until their memory faded into oblivion.

What generally becomes merchandisable are those media products—of book, film, TV, and game origin—that can be transformed into other concepts and merchandise. Licensors and media hypesters have no trouble extending the media lives of phenomenally successful franchises like *Chicken Soup . . . , Teletubbies,* and Beanie Babies. The rationale is, if you loved the book—or the movie—then you will buy the peripheral merchandising. Children couldn't get enough of *The Little Mermaid* and *Toy Story,* and it was reflected by their parents' purchase of millions of dollars of socks, underwear, place mats and lunch boxes, and action figure dolls.

A more recent phenomenon has been the merchandising exploitation of the incredible bestselling *Harry Potter* series by J. K. Rowling. The four published books to date have captivated children and their parents around the world, to the point where the books recently appeared on the *New York Times* fiction bestseller list as numbers 1, 2, 3, and 4. The *Times* created a new children's bestseller list in response to the *Harry Potter* phenomenon. Predictably, the licensed spin-off products are coming—a Warner Bros. film (the first of a series, of course), toys, video games, and action figures. *Harry Potter* is coming to your neighborhood—in every kind of form and format.

Sometimes the exploitative breakout is in reverse. *Myst* began as a computer game, *Dilbert* as a comic strip. The now-celebrated *Furby* animal toy that speaks multilingual gibberish is being morphed into books and other merchandise. Publishers are also buying brand names to develop book and other ancillary products. Recent examples include a Cheerios Play Book and a Lionel Train book series coming from Simon & Schuster. Scholastic has licensed 2 Grrris, a gift line, to produce *What a Friend* and *Hello Gorgeous*—two of the line's cult catch phrases. And there is also *The Oreo Cookie Counting Book,* and a *Sun•Maid Raisins Play Book.*

Today, the hype and the proliferating licensing extravaganza are carefully planned and orchestrated from the outset. They are well-conceived campaigns to establish brand-name recognition and sell the media product in all possible configurations. If the poster is a natural extension of film or book, then so is the twelve-month calendar, the Page-a-Day calendar . . . and perhaps a date book. How many products will serve rather than satiate the marketplace is often dependent on the content viability of the original idea. For the bestseller or blockbuster, there never seem to be too few, but there are often too many, ancillary products.

Where and how do *you* begin this merchandising process? One media product, usually the original, has to be significantly successful and to have evoked a sales response from the public. As noted previously in the example of *Buffy the Vampire Slayer,* the initial movie did not generate merchandising dollars, but the subsequent television series did. Luck and timing are again factors in calculating a successful licensing campaign.

You should be cognizant of the media marketing possibilities for your book or idea and be knowledgeable about how you will reach these markets. Who will conceive your products? Who will orchestrate these licensing sales for you? You may have sold all media rights, in which case the company that is exploiting your film (e.g., Warner Bros. for the *Harry Potter* series) will also control the merchandising. There are also licensing specialists who can find the appropriate buyers in the apparel field, for toys and games, for calendars, posters, and paper and party products, and in the new media world of electronic and digital merchandising. They can be found at the various licensing and merchandising conventions, or usually from word-of-mouth recommendations from your writer colleagues.

A licensing agent or company can protect your idea and can identify and sell to the most suitable markets for your particular product. Many specialize in exploiting proprietary creations that may include toys, inventions, games, hobbies, animated logos and/or products, stories, and other unique brand-name ideas. They generally receive a commission in the range of 15 percent. There is also an annual national licensing show held every June at the Javits Center in New York City, which is sponsored by LIMA (Licensing International Merchandising Association), the official U.S. licensing organization. Your publisher, your agent, and your TV or film company will invariably know the licensing agents and marketers and how to navigate those ancillary opportunities.

If you want to create the next merchandising bonanza, you have to hang around the marketplace. If you have kids, you can't help observing (or buying) the latest fads, games, and tchotchkes. The licensing campaign is orchestrated to overwhelm and oversaturate us with derivative products. List all the spin-off merchandising your idea could possibly become. Can, or should you, solicit Mattel, Hasbro Toys, General Mills, or McDonald's to consider your product? If you don't have a book or movie coming out, it will be more difficult. Your chances of licensing success will be greatly enhanced if your created concept will be launched in some media form or format. You have to begin somewhere, and the bandwagon effect can eventuate if success is achieved in any one market. Remember the lessons of Barney and *Chicken Soup*.

A further word of optimistic advice: Assume that your idea will be successful, and be ready—via your own efforts or through your licensing rep—to launch a merchandising assault on prospective buyers. Be attuned to signals of word-of-mouth interest from kids, their parents, and the marketplace in general that you've got the next Pokémon or *Star Wars*.

When a media phenomenon strikes—like *Harry Potter,* or *The Blair Witch Project,* or *Don't Sweat the Small Stuff*—the merchandisers will find you. If you create it, they will come. Everybody desires the decal rights to extraordinarily successful media hits.

If you are actively creating licensable projects or just serendipitously happen to fall into this world of merchandising mania, you will want to know the deal and the ramifications thereof. The terms and royalties or residuals all vary in the different licensing arrangements. How and when you get paid will be an additional variable. Are the licensed products sold on consignment, like books and records, thus keyed to net sales? If you sold merchandising rights for socks, are the sneakers part of the deal? Are calendars and posters aligned together? Know what you have, what you have sold, and who owns your rights. Usually the publishing contract will divide publishing and merchandising rights. The book publisher will retain the standard book club, serial, and audio markets, but the author will hold all film, electronic, and merchandising rights. The film company that acquires world movie rights will usually control the merchandising sales as an integral part of that deal.

One piece of merchandising sells another. The kid who has the game and the action figures also wants the clothes and the shoes. He covets the complete set of *Lion King* or *Star Wars* collectibles. *Chicken Soup* overflows to more *Chicken Soup*. *Furbys* give birth to *Furby Babies*. You can *Find Waldo* in a book, a game, a poster, or a puzzle. The merchandising horizon is unlimited and open for new creative ventures.

When I was a neophyte, licensing books to new untapped markets, I discovered something totally unique. There was a company called Oh Dawn that bought the serialization rights to interesting excerptable books and reproduced them on rolls of toilet paper. Beyond the jokes that it was a total wipeout, the experiment worked as a new ancillary vehicle for the licensing of print media ideas. There was a further irony. I met the proprietor of Oh Dawn years later on the West Coast. She was Dawn Steel, who became the first female head of a major motion picture studio—Paramount Pictures. We became West Coast friends and shared many a media concept over the years. We laughed and appreciated the fact that we had effected an unusual licensing deal many years back.

Licensing merchandising can be innovative, fun, and very lucrative. It depends on the seminal media product and how it performs in the consumer marketplace. Some media concepts become sweatshirts and CD-ROMs and posters. Many don't.

It is worth the endeavor, worth the exploitation. There are invariably movies that remain unseen, and books that are unread. But someone, somewhere may be wearing the T-shirt of Austin Powers.

The Internet explosion has provided unlimited opportunities for authors, screenwriters, and idea innovators. The traditional and long-standing methods of conception, production, and distribution have been favorably distorted by the scope of the Internet. The initial results have been instant and dramatic. The future possibilities are endless. Bestselling books and hit media projects are being integrated into the Worldwide Web. The cult TV show *South Park* is being converted into a short cartoon series to appear on the Web. It will be introduced on Shockwave.com, an entertainment Web site initiated by Macromedia. Other products and entertainment concepts are debuting on the Internet, including Stephen King's serial novel, *The PLANT,* which he sold for $1 an installment on the honor system.

The emergence of the Internet has transformed the ways we conceive, record, and store ideas. Our manuscripts and creative ideas are typed into the computer, stored indefinitely, and edited on-line. They can be printed out, duplicated, changed, and transmitted to another person or multiple persons.

It is "in our machine"—to rewrite or send out or save as we wish.

Of course, there are still some purists, as there always are, who will not adopt twenty-first-century innovations. Recently one of them—an elderly lady—brought her worn-out typewriter ribbon to an Office Depot and asked the young clerk for "a new one of these." He came back a few minutes later and said with some bewilderment, "What is it?"

Once your novel or screenplay gets out of the machine or is typed with the new ribbon, myriad opportunities now exist for Internet exploitation. It is anticipated that approximately half of all books sold in America five years from now will be purchased from on-line retailers like Amazon.com, Barnes & Noble.com, and other competitors. The retail store marketplace will have more of a salon ambience, with coffee bars, author readings, and live seminars. Small independent bookstores may inevitably become obsolete. Every retailer, distributor, and publisher is actively seeking strategic alliances with electronic and digital partners. Random House has bought a major interest in Xlibris.com, which enables authors to self-publish electronic books, and has also established a digital unit, At Random. Time Warner has announced plans to launch iPublish, converting existing publications to electronic format. Other major publishers are adopting E-book publishing formats, and are now publishing their brand-name authors in E-book as well as traditional book formats.

The new millennium will witness the convergence of software and hardware at a proliferating rate. Although the content may not change appreciably, the mode of delivery inevitably will. Books will be made available via new electronic wireless devices, and any—and all—backlist or out-of-print titles can be printed in some readable format within twenty-four hours.

Electronic books (E-books) can now be recorded digitally and downloaded on-line, making it unlikely that individual books need ever go out of print. This means enormous savings in not having to print or distribute books or pay for returns of unwanted books. Published and unpublished authors will now be able to become instant "virtual vanity" publishers and make their works downloadable and available via the Internet. And, as prognosticated in an earlier chapter, brand-name authors could choose this publication and distribution route, bypassing the "bricks and mortar" retailers to sell exclusively on-line and eliminate their traditional publishers. New merchandising scenarios seem to materialize every day.

Neophyte authors, screenwriters, and other creators will be able to employ the latest technological advances of printing on demand. Books, pamphlets, monographs, clinical papers, movie treatments, and other creative writing can be printed as needed, and it will not be necessary to print and bind excessive quantities of stored inventory. Single copies can instantly be made available to consumers who will pay for this downloading privilege. No manufacturing, no costly shipments and mailings, no warehousing. Ironically, self-published books that were impossible to sell to Barnes & Noble, Borders, or Amazon will now be accessible on their sites.

The retail stores will also be capable of producing an instant book on demand. Barnes & Noble has recently bought a major share of iUniverse.com, a print-on-demand publisher. It will make available new and out-of-print books via its Web site and on the Barnes & Noble on-line bookselling site. Your previously out-of-print book or your new manuscript can now be made available via the Internet in approximately one month from delivery of editorial materials. Barnes & Noble has additionally effected an arrangement with IBM to provide print-on-demand technology for its distribution sites, to convert digitally produced books into print-format versions. Another innovator, netLibrary, sells collections of digital books to libraries. The traditional print publishers are preparing to digitize their backlists to compete in the new E-world of paperless publishing. Component parts and sections of books—predominantly in the travel, cookbook, and how-to categories—will be downloaded into customized books, sort of à la carte publishing, similar to the mix of "greatest song hits."

An innovative Silicon Valley company, Fatbrain.com, has just been launched to sell a creator's "eMatter." Fatbrain will design an Amazon-type page for your work (for reasonable setup fees) and make it available for downloading. They will collect the payments and split the profits with you, the author, on a fifty-fifty split.

The more extensive costs will be to disseminate these future publications by linking to or advertising on other Web sites, the bigger the better. A recently launched division of Ingram Distributors in Nashville, Tennessee—Lightning Print—can digitize any book and create an immediate edition for consumers. The book is always in print, and copies—single or multiple—are always available. Several publishers announced strategic alliances with another Ingram E-book and printing-on-demand entity, Lightning Source. Lightning will become those publishers' primary digital fulfillment company. Additionally, the Rowman & Littlefield Group, which publishes academic titles, announced the first on-demand printing facility at its printer, Edwards Brothers. Printing on demand will transform the publishing industry and inspire a new generation of instant and virtual publishers. The real challenge will be to evoke a consumer response and find a commercially viable market for single unknown books.

On your own initiative, you will be able to write and publish your own book with an investment of less than $500.

The process is manageable, quick, and relatively inexpensive. The dissemination is difficult. Once you've created a new E-book, the creative challenge will be to get listed and recognized on another site more popular than your own.

A mention or endorsement on the iVillage or Oxygen networks could be a catalyst to selling your book. Additionally, you could promote your creative work or book via on-line chat rooms (interactive communication), author interviews and readings on the Internet, and on-line seminars.

Another innovation that is soon coming to your small screen is the Microsoft Reader. It is the first reading software that features a font of extremely clear type. It will afford readers or writers an opportunity to reproduce or publish writing via their personal computers, desktops, or laptops. If you are the creator or author of E-book ideas and manuscripts—or just an interested reader—the availability of instant entertainment and information is only a click or two away.

The E-publishing world of the immediate future will facilitate the creation and dissemination of books and ideas. Quantities can range from one copy to thousands of copies. Additionally, there is now an E-book that can be downloaded into an E-book reader, featuring a viewer approximately the size of a book page. The new Rocket E-book is able to hold ten downloaded books and thousands of pages. The Glassbook reader can also download an E-book. Another innovator, Peanut Press, sells digital books for reading on palmtop computers. The advantages of E-books are that they can be linked to the Web—either wired or wireless. Now you no longer have to pack heavy hardcover books to read on your next vacation in the Hamptons or in the south of France. They can come with you on your downloadable viewer, if that is how you choose to read.

The technological advances of E-books and publishing on demand have already changed the dynamics and economics of the media world and accelerated the speed of bringing books and ideas to the marketplace.

The new or virtual author and creator or the E-publisher will also be able to utilize the worldwide Internet mechanism to sell and promote products. Aside from the ability to print on demand and to sell via other sites, the chat room has opened up a new promotional opportunity.

If you go on-line and click onto the Internet, you can go into a chat room and communicate electronically with one person or groups of people. An author, an educator, or a guru in a particular field can impart wisdom to a large multitude via the chat room forum. Questions can be asked and answered (by typing electronically), and information and ideas can be transmitted to people in any major city in the world. In my recent appearances as the "book guru" guest in the iVillage national chat room, I was awestruck by the unique qualities of this new mode of dissemination. While I was conducting this forum in my home in Los Angeles, the host was in Portland, Oregon, my facilitator was in Indianapolis, and the audience consisted of people from every region of the country in every time zone, all communicating and discussing books from the comfort of our own homes.

This form of communication will only grow in usage and popularity in today's media world. Through "collaborative filtering," we can process and assimilate insider information that has been filtered through hundreds of people and sources to provide a myriad of condensed ideas. It has become a human search engine for ideas, facts, and opinions.

A further Web extension for authors and creators is the marketing concept of "bundling"—selling multiple products that are related and brand-name packaged—and "backroom"—where all the products that are bundled are made available for Web purchase via credit card. You can build your site, preach your message in a chat room, create a backroom sales apparatus, link on to Ingram, Barnes & Noble, Amazon, or another corporate or media Web site—and become an instant author and publisher. If you are not a self-published author or neophyte creator but are fortunate enough to have signed a major contract with a Simon & Schuster, Sony Columbia, or HBO—you still have the potential prospect of developing ancillary or supplemental sales via the Internet and its proliferating marketing extensions. Your creative concept can be linked to your publisher, your film or TV buyer, your mail-order company, and any site that can effectively promote and sell your book.

Another Web window is the emergence of on-line seminars, a concept innovated by author and filmmaker Stephen Smoke and others. Whether you are a beginning author or a bestselling brand name, you can create on-line seminars on your book or media topic. Once you've written and published your product—be it book or film, musical or spoken rendition—you can produce a corresponding seminar that allows you to record a lecture on your chosen subject. It may last a half hour or an hour, and it will be disseminated on the Internet. Thousands or potentially millions of people throughout the world may view it. After you have delivered your creative seminar, you have the option of expanding your future messages or seminars on your Web site, selling your derivative products in your backroom, or offering your media products via Web sales—on your site or elsewhere.

One curious problem has pervaded this explosive new industry: the purchase and use of "domain names" for Web sites have become a very competitive, avaricious side business. All the generic names have been bought for significant fees. Weather.com, Drugs.com, Toys.com *ad extendum* have been acquired and sometimes resold. Chances are that your name has not been taken or sold, but there is every likelihood that your company or your brand name is an integral part of someone else's domain.

Recently, when I was a principal in a major television special and merchandising/Internet exploitation, we found that *our* domain name had already been taken. Our two options were to buy the name from the incumbent (they keep turning down our escalating offers) or create a similar but different identity. Start early to lock in your domain name. It can get rough out there in cyberspace.

The possibilities of the Web are changing and growing almost on a daily basis. Creators, inventors, authors, designers, writers, and mediaphiles are linking, hyperlinking, digitizing, interacting, and downloading. A new lexicon serves the new electronic digital world. The important message for the beginner is to study this new medium and become versed in the possibilities of Internet marketing. See how your project can relate to someone else's site or someone else's marketing vehicle.

The new technology provides advanced hardware ranging from our home and office machines to our traveling laptops to the newly innovated wireless Web. It is inevitable that our electronic media machine of the future will be compact, portable, wireless, capable of Web access, E-book reading and downloading, phone and fax messages, cable and television viewing, and E-commerce for any product at any time. As writers and creators, we can bring our book or concept to the marketplace and create numerous scenarios for selling it through the E-commerce mechanism. Whatever print or visual medium once existed will be supplemented by the scope and magnitude of the Internet. It is incumbent upon us to become educated about these unlimited possibilities and to gain a marketing edge in this new media world.

An alternative electronic medium, primarily for the youth market, is the almost kaleidoscopic galaxy of CD-ROMs and interactive games. The pioneers in this electronic world are Sega and Nintendo. The Sega Genesis console has typically been oriented to teens, while Nintendo is more alluring to the younger set. The most recent state of the art is the Sega Dreamcast console, retailing in the $200 price range.

Millions of dollars have been spent on the accompanying dazzling games, whose bestsellers include names like *Sonic the Hedgehog, Mortal Kombat,* and *Trick Style.* Often the CD-ROM or electronic game spin-offs emanate from intergalactic or fast-paced action films. *Star Wars, Armageddon,* and *The Sixth Sense* are prototypical licensing examples. And in the exploding world of ancillary spin-off products, *Pokémon* now features a battery-operated handheld machine to complement the Nintendo game, the trading cards, and now—the movie.

Aside from the electronic game crazes, CD-ROMs are a significant educational tool, featuring book-derived materials, classic children's stories, and ideas

and subjects that are educationally challenging and instructive. Predictably, every academic discipline is a
potential CD-ROM disk. All previously published
books pertaining to information and learning are candidates for transformation into CD-ROMs.

We have become a digitized society. Almost two
hundred million people are now on the Internet worldwide, approximately half of them in the United States.
For the beginning writer and media creator, there has
never been a more challenging or promising time.
Books, treatments, and concepts will continue to be
published, filmed, licensed, and merchandised—but
they will also be *up*linked and *down*loaded. In the new
electronic world of creativity and commerce, Internet-
working will be the prevailing way we conduct our
businesses and live our lives.

First-time authors and creators are invariably thrilled when a potential deal materializes for them. It is often the culmination of a long, arduous, and intensely creative journey. Although we are anxious to sign that initial contract, it is of paramount importance that we have the proper representation, negotiate the best deal we can make, and sign an agreement that is favorable and faithful to our interests. No contract is ever consummated with the expectation that it will end up in litigation. We generally negotiate and sign in good faith. What ultimately evolves is often a different scenario. Then the fine print in our contract comes into play.

It is incumbent upon *you* to understand the deal you make and the agreement that memorializes it. It is also imperative that you be absolutely cognizant of the rights you are granting. There have been innumerable cases of motion picture, television, or electronic rights being mistakenly assigned to a book publisher. They are different media and should be negotiated separately.

Unless you have particular expertise, your media contracts should be handled by a capable attorney or agent who is familiar with the particular type of negotiation and contract in question. This agreement is too important to you and your creative career to relegate it to your brother-in-law who sells insurance or a friend who knows real estate law. You need an expert, someone who knows the intricacies of the book, film, or digital contract.

The standard publication contract with Random House or Penguin or with most book publishers features numerous boilerplate (standard) clauses that are not negotiable by the neophyte. They generally relate to warranties and indemnities and require you to assert legally that you have not written or submitted any defamatory, libelous, or plagiaristic material—and that you will indemnify your publisher against all claims and actions that could constitute a breach of your representations and warranties. In other words, you are holding the publisher harmless from liability if there is anything libelous or litigable in your work. Fair and equitable enough.

The salient negotiable points in a book contract encompass the "grant of publication rights," the advance, and subsequent royalties. There are standard royalty formulas in the industry—usually 10 percent for the first 5,000 copies sold, 12.5 percent in the next 5,000 copies sold, and 15 percent thereafter on all hardcover editions; 8 percent on the first 150,000 copies sold and 10 percent thereafter on mass-market paperback editions; and approximately 7.5 percent on the first 15,000 or 20,000 copies sold with escalated royalties thereafter for trade paperback editions.

Royalties or ancillary rights earnings are only paid *after* the advance has been earned back—and royalties are for *net* sales, after returns are accounted for. If 10,000 copies of a book are distributed and 3,000 are returned, the publisher's obligation is to pay royalties on the net sales of 7,000 copies. Additionally, the publisher will hold a "reserve" against those returns for the first two or three royalty periods. The reserve, usually about 20 percent, is in anticipation that there will be initial returns of a newly distributed book.

Other contractual clauses include the world territories in which your book can be sold and/or licensed; the proposed delivery date of your manuscript; option on future works (which should always be "on terms mutually agreed upon"). Also, pay particular attention to the subsidiary rights granted: what rights you are licensing to the publisher and what you are retaining as author. In most circumstances, and especially when you are represented by a skillful agent, you will hold back all motion picture, television, cable, and, in some cases, merchandising or electronic rights. They should not be an integral part of your publication contract; you are generally free to license those potentially lucrative rights separately.

A word of caution when you finalize your publication agreement. Make sure you are signing with a reputable publisher who will not only adhere to the terms of the contract but is likely to remain in business and successfully bring your manuscript to publication. There have been numerous instances of houses with a dubious publishing record and an erratic cash flow predictably defaulting into Chapter 11 bankruptcy. Even such a major publisher as HarperCollins recently cancelled over a hundred existing contracts as a way of substantially reducing its publishing commitments.

Know your publisher, know its recent track record, and be attuned to its strengths and weaknesses in launching and sustaining bestsellers or reasonably successful books. What you can favorably negotiate now will be to your benefit once your book is ultimately published.

Motion picture and television deals are even more intricate, and an adroit agent in the field or a savvy entertainment attorney is necessary here as well. These contracts can run from fifty to a hundred pages, with boilerplate clauses that will confound you. The key negotiating points must reflect what you are getting up front, at each stage of the development or production process, and what your backend participation will be. Option money or front-end money is yours to keep if the project does not materialize or finds its way into turnaround (oblivion). If you are participating in points or percentages of profit and backend payments, it is almost a certainty that you will be a *net* participant. The *gross* players are the few stars whose names go before the title, and those directors, producers, and authors who are legendary, successful, or both. Tom Cruise, Julia Roberts, and Martin Scorsese get gross points. You will receive net points—after the film or TV show has earned back its expenses.

A typical film deal will involve step payments— monies paid at each step of development; for example, on signing, on completion of treatment, on completion of first draft and first polish, on start of principal photography (when the picture is ready to be filmed), and on release of the motion picture. Your backend points and percentages of net profit will kick in *after* the film earns out its budget, which includes its costs—above (the stars) and below the line (actual cost of filming), distribution fees, extraneous studio fees, prints and advertising, the interest on that accumulated cost, and whatever else creative movie accountants may add to the film mix.

It is crucial to your immediate cash flow and to your continuing movie career that you understand at what stages you will be paid and what is required of you to trigger that payment. Invariably, the motion picture company that buys the rights to production will be acquiring television, dramatic, and merchandising rights as well. That is OK—as long as they are paying for those potentially valuable rights and not just retaining them for an indefinite period. The word *forever* sometimes pops up in these fifty-page legal treatises. If there is an ultimate reversion—to you—you want all your rights back, all those that were granted in the original contract.

If you are a participant in net points and your share is 5 percent, will you receive 5 percent of 100 percent of net profits or (assuming the studio or film financier gets 50 percent) 5 percent of 50 percent of profits? Know, before signing, what your actual percentage will be. It is a moot point for films that don't earn—but megadollars for blockbuster hits that do. If you are fortunate enough to have been allocated *gross* points, your percentage share will come off the top—before deductions of any kind.

For every $8 paid for a ticket at the box office, the theater retains half. The rest gets remitted back to the studio and is proportioned among producers, financiers, director, stars—and the "running budget." What you receive at the outset is very meaningful because you will have been paid, no matter what eventuates.

Credits are also important to your film future. Shared credits reduce your clout and credibility. If your name is totally removed as writer or creator, it could be detrimental to your subsequent endeavors. The credit is your entree to your next project. People in the motion picture business are impressed with track records and success stories. What you have previously accomplished is likely to accrue greater dollars for you the next film go-around.

Television contracts and dealings are similarly intricate. This is primarily due to the variance among different kinds of TV formats. Your creative role and input could range from conceiving the story or idea to writing one show, producing a series, being hired to write all episodes, or serving as a creative consultant, a contributor, or as an "original creator"—à la Rod Serling. You and your expert negotiator should be aware of your role and the length of your tenure and involvement. If you had created *Mash* or *Cheers* and were an income participant in all airings, remakes, sequels, and syndications—you would be extremely rich today.

Once you know the envisioned TV format and what

"they" are buying, you and your agent or attorney can negotiate on that premise. For long-form MOWs, dramas, series, or strip or game shows, you will most likely receive some money up front and participation percentages each step along the way. Since many TV concepts or pilots traditionally don't materialize, what you receive at the outset of the deal can be very important to you. If your concept ultimately gets to syndication (domestically or globally), there can be lucrative residuals for years, or forever. These have materialized for very successful long-running TV series or entertainment fare like *People's Court* or *Wheel of Fortune*.

Be careful in your television deal that you are receiving percentages of everything that ultimately airs on television. You must necessarily cover each contingency that may evolve. You want to participate in earnings if your special segues into a series or your one-shot idea becomes an ongoing show for syndication. In my present involvement as an executive producer for the television project *Glamour Girls of the Century*, our projected formats are different in each country. Some markets desire a one-and-a-half-hour special with sequels to follow. Some prefer a thirteen-week syndicated series—an hour per week. There is also speculation about an annual *Glamour Girls* awards show. We had to be contractually prepared for all formats and all contingencies.

We were also prepared for multimedia and merchandising exploitation à la *The Elvis Files*. The creatively clever Richard Leto, with whom I worked on *Elvis*, again was controlling the master switchboard for 800- and 900-number call-ins. We anticipated over a million calls—on a worldwide basis. Additionally, this time around we could utilize the Internet via our *Glamour Girls* Web site to sell backroom merchandising and our other media products. Since our TV show and its related ancillary merchandise were derived from a successfully published book, we were orchestrating total media saturation.

If your media product is licensed for apparel, toys, or other items, your negotiating should key to these determinants. What are they selling? At what price? How many will they produce, or what do they anticipate selling initially? What is your royalty or percentage rate?

If you licensed sweatshirt rights to your slogan, title, or brand name, for example, you might be told that projected sales were 30,000 shirts at $20 each. If you were to receive 10 percent, your advance or initial share should approximate $60,000:

$$30,000 \times \$20 = \$600,000 \times .10\% = \$60,000.$$

If you sell or license electronic, CD-ROM, or Internet rights, you can apply the same formulas—money up front plus royalty percentages after the advance is earned out. When the original creators of *Superman* sold all their rights, little did they or their estates realize how lucrative digital and media rights (not yet invented) would become circa the year 2000.

There are generally a number of basic questions to ask when licensing or selling a media property. You must ascertain the following information before consummating your deal:

1. What is the acquiring entity going to do with the property? How, where, when will they sell it, publish it, produce it?
2. What rights are they acquiring?
3. What is the contemplated retail price?
4. What advances or up-front monies will be paid?
5. What is the royalty or percentage rate?
6. What are the projected sales?
7. What are your contractual obligations as writer/creator?

All media negotiations involve similar contract components. You want to know what you are granting and how and when you will be paid. Suppositional or unclear answers to the above questions will most likely cause problems as the creative project comes to fruition. If specific terms are not clearly delineated at the outset, they will not be interpreted in your favor if a dispute subsequently arises. The handshake or verbal deal will certainly not be beneficial to you. Get it all in writing and make sure the salient deal points are understood by everyone. And again, be very familiar with the media arena you are about to enter. Learn to understand the film, TV, publishing, and/or electronic/ Internet business, and follow the successes—or failures—of individual projects. It will be meaningful to your ongoing education in the mercurial world of media exploitation.

Lawsuits arise from misunderstandings and misinterpretations. There are thousands of attorneys in Beverly Hills and Hollywood. They are ubiquitous because there are celebrities who need their egos defined and massaged. The legal route is often the vehicle to settling grudges and stating just who you are. "They didn't fulfill the terms of the contract" is a lament often heard from artists and authors, novelists, and neophytes. Something went awry in the interpretive process, even though the original parties thought they were adhering to the same contract. The axiom for *you* to remember is: Close a *good* deal. Don't make a *bad* deal.

Authors often decry the lack of promotional effort by their publishers. Screenwriters can be disappointed. Your expectations should be hopeful but realistic. There are many writers and creators who have continually renewed their associations with their publishers and studios. Author Pat Conroy (*The Prince of Tides*) and editor Nan Talese have worked together throughout his bestselling career. Stephen Spielberg has enjoyed a long and mutually fulfilling relationship with Universal Pictures over several decades. Success often breeds more success—on the bestseller lists, on the charts, at the box office.

Whatever your creative aspirations, whatever your success, you will feel more secure and confident if you have efficiently attended to the "business of the business." You will have *earned* the rewards and royalties of film fame or bestsellerdom.

Success leads to sequels. If your first book, screenplay, or creative endeavor is a hit, a sequel or a series or a prospective franchise will surely follow. As we noted previously, Sue Grafton has an imaginative success formula that will ultimately translate into twenty-six "alphabet" books. Her latest bestseller, *O Is for Outlaw,* means that she's more than halfway through that alphabet already. Janet Evanovich features a similar formula, with her popular ongoing series *One for the Money, Two for the Dough*—and the obvious sequels to come. *Don't Sweat the Small Stuff, Politically Correct Bedtime Stories,* and Margaret Truman's *Murder in* (some Washington, D.C., landmark) series will be generating sequels for years to come.

When I was president of Pinnacle Books, we orchestrated series publications by the numbers. The very successful *Destroyer, Executioner,* and *Hornblower* series were mass-produced as *Destroyer* number 29, 30, 31, and indefinitely. The marketplace covets and demands *more* of what it has previously enjoyed and what it deems successful. If a film works commercially at the box office, it will lead to the obligatory *Rocky II, III . . .* until it reaches a saturation point. *Amityville Horror* begets more *Horror*. *Planet of the Apes* spawns *Return to Planet of the Apes*. *Scream* becomes *Scream II* and *III* and onward. *Die Hard—Dies Harder—Dies Hardest*.

In the juvenile world, the *Nancy Drew* and *Hardy Boys* series have been continuing over many a young person's lifetime. *If You Give a Mouse a Cookie* segued into *If You Give a Kid a Pancake*—and beyond. The already canonized *Harry Potter* is projected as a nine-book episodic adventure.

Although most enduring series have started out as serendipitous successes, many are planned as series from their conceptual stages. *The Baby-Sitters Club* and *Goosebumps* were orchestrated that way with all the attendant hype and promotion at the launch. The publishers were intent on ensuring initial success and prolonging the commercial life of the series. If it worked, they were prepared to publish and sequelize for as long as the public responded favorably. If number one does not materialize, as we demonstrated with the *Destroyer* series movie (*Remo Williams*), sequels are unlikely.

The challenge is to achieve a media success and keep it going forever. *Chicken Soup for the Soul* has literally become a franchised enterprise—like Mc-

Donald's or Kentucky Fried Chicken. The original books were authored by Jack Canfield and Mark Victor Hansen and published by small Florida health publishers Health Communications, now HCI. As the series flourished to incredible bestselling proportions, the authors became "executive producers" or licensers of that franchise. Writers and authors were hired to create and develop individual products for particular niches—*Chicken Soup for Golfers* and so on. It was promoted as a generic franchise as the soup series overflowed into the media marketplace, becoming calendars and audiotapes and licensed products and ultimately a television series, sponsored by—Campbell's Soup, of course.

The *Dummies* series and the *Idiots* guides are cleverly marketed concepts that can be extended indefinitely. Once they proved themselves as authoritative manuals, their sponsors could publish a *Dummies Guide* to every conceivable subject. They have become recognizable brand names with labels and logos that register as a seal of approval and acceptance. Fell's *Know It All* series is enjoying a successful launch as a competitive franchise of books. The similar titles, the size, the typeface and design are all carefully conceived to achieve brand-name identity, not unlike Oreo Cookies, Ritz Crackers, and other supermarketed products.

Random Acts of Kindness began as an inspiration and a single book—and became a worldwide movement. The simple words *Practice Random Acts of Kindness and Senseless Acts of Beauty* were scrawled on a restaurant place mat—and almost overnight were transformed into bestselling books and by-products. More importantly, the sentence became a credo and was printed on bumper stickers around the world. It was more than a book series or a concept. The words inspired an outbreak of kindness, and their message became contagious.

Kids' Random Acts of Kindness soon followed, and there were calendars and tapes and journals. A TV series was in the offing. What started out as a slogan soon evolved into a media celebration of ancillary products. There seemed to be no limitations on *Random Acts of Kindness*. And we the public were the beneficiaries.

Television thrives on continuity series. It is the lifeline of the TV medium. A *Cheers,* a *Seinfeld,* a *Friends* can run for seven years and then be sold for worldwide syndication—to run almost forever. Such has been the case with *I Love Lucy* and *Mary Tyler Moore* reruns. They will continue to endure and be watched. Since television is dependent on advertising revenues, serial success guarantees the continuity of ads and the perpetual "buy-in." Some fifteen to twenty-five million people at one time may watch a weekly show, as compared with 15,000 to 25,000 copies sold of a moderately successful book. Each new TV program perpetuates the life and commerce of that particular series, just as the book series depends on the latest Sue Grafton to sell the backlist, the entire early alphabet of her novels.

Similarly, a game or toy product needs initial consumer acceptance to establish brand recognition. When and if it catches on, the spin-off products can eventuate. We know and love Barney, Teletubbies, and Thomas the Tank, and we feel secure buying their ancillary media configurations. Children want much more of their youthful icons. They are rarely satiated.

Once, the inundation of licensed products was a chance happening. Today, when a *Little Mermaid* or *Toy Story* or *Star Wars* is launched, the media hype is orchestrated as a carefully conceived marketing plan. Sell the T-shirts, the audio, the place mats, the apparel, and the toys because everyone will have heard of the movie. In some instances, after the movie and the merchandise have come and gone, the original creative idea evolves into a new medium. *Ragtime* went from book to Broadway, with a movie in between. *The Lion King* was transformed into an extraordinary

Broadway musical with a long life expectancy. The show and the shirts will sell forever.

Often, the series is perpetuated by its protagonist. Kinsey Millhone, Sue Grafton's indomitable heroine, appears in all of her novels. So does James Patterson's detective creation, Alex Cross. P. D. James's celebrated Inspector Dalgliesh solves all of her bestselling mystery yarns. And, of course, young sorcerer Harry Potter emerges again and again in his now-famous adventure series.

Even the death of the author or creator need not interfere with extension of the series. The lives of numerous popular authors have been extended in continuing book publications. Ian Fleming (James Bond's creator), the Western writer Louis L'Amour, and the infectious gothic author V. C. Andrews all passed on years ago, but their literary output goes on and on. Someone writing in a similar if not identical style is hired by the estate and publisher to continue the celebrated author's publication life. Fans are often impervious to the fact that their favorite authors have long since departed. Memories of them remain green, and their books remain in print and in perpetual publication.

The successful nonfiction concept is invariably repeated on a formula basis. *Men Are from Mars, Women*

Are from Venus continued into subsequent books that included *Men Are from Mars, Children Are from Heaven.* *The 7 Habits of Highly Successful People* is extended to *Families,* and *Passages* leads to *New Passages.* *The First Twelve Months of Life* naturally grows into *The Second Twelve Months of Life,* and beyond.

Peter Mayle's delightful travel essays have enriched three books—*A Year in Provence, Toujours Provence,* and *Encore Provence.*

Television is cognizant of the spin-off philosophy. *60 Minutes* is thinly recreated as *48 Hours* on another evening. *Jeopardy* quizzes and *Trivial Pursuit* games are reworked into younger-age versions. And the movies will continually repeat a formula concept until every box-office dollar is squeezed out of it. The marketing rationale always reflects the rules of familiarity. We tend to buy and come back to what we know—what is familiar to us. Then too, if a media project is an unqualified hit, it creates a bandwagon effect. We desire what everybody else is buying and talking about.

It is incumbent on *you,* the creator, to conceive an idea that could have sequel potential as well as ancillary exploitation. An unusual character, a charismatic hero or heroine, a "warm and fuzzy" doll could be the early inspiration for spin-off franchises. One Pokémon, one Barney could break out into a rash of media merchandise. What does the marketplace need now? What will replace Furby or Beanie Babies? What will be the next *Bridges of Madison County,* the next *Chicken Soup* phenomenon? Think in terms of a franchisable idea and how you can sequelize and exploit your concept.

Study the marketing and advertising campaigns of these successful products to ascertain why they worked. Those empirical data will be of great value to you, although much still will be dependent on the elements of luck and timing.

If you have previously sold a book for publication, or a film or game or TV show, and you have achieved a modicum of success, you and/or your advisers may be contemplating that sequel. There are a number of key questions that should be addressed before orchestrating such an encore.

1. *Was the initial book or product* really *a success? Or was it a hype that didn't sell as well as expected?*

   All too often bestseller wannabes are generously distributed with all attendant promotion, but they fail to materialize as bestsellers and are returned in abundance. Similarly, overhyped movies fail to attract box-office viewers and languish in the theaters.

2. *Was the product or lead character aptly named and defined?*

It's hard to imagine James Bond by any other name, but Victor Hugo's epic character Quasimodo didn't translate well commercially as a licensed action figure.

3. *Do I repeat publication or media development with the same company?*

How compatible and successful you were *together* is the key to your sequel involvement.

4. *Do I change agents or representatives?*

Not unless you are unhappy with their contribution.

5. *Should I alter my package or logo or design?*

If you have established an identifiable brand-name look, stay with it. If it can be overhauled or enhanced visually, change the image.

6. *Which contractual clauses were to my benefit? Which ones would I delete or alter?*

Invariably, particularly with moneymaking ventures, there are contract clauses that prove to be unfavorable to you. If you can change them, do so.

7. *What new markets are worth exploring and exploiting this time around?*

Some may be newly innovated—like Internet

chat rooms or E-publishing. Some may be licensing extensions—calendars to place mats to greeting cards.

8. *What are the areas that worked out well for you the first time around? What didn't work out well?* Make the adjustments accordingly.

Once you have answers to these relevant questions, begin to plan and effect the sequel to your initial success.

If *your* preparation meets *your* opportunity, and luck factors into the equation, you will have achieved significant media and publication results. I believe it *will* and *can* happen for you.

I'm rooting for you, and I'm predicting your success. I want to hear all about it. Contact me via E-mail—scorwin844@aol.com.

I wish you bestselling books, blockbuster movies, and TV shows that run into lifetime syndication. I wish you popular games and toys, your own brand-name T-shirt and emblem, and a new world of E-commerce and Web discoveries. You will have earned it; you will have worked for it. You will have been read, listened to, seen, and probably downloaded. You will have enjoyed the new media millennium experience—and you will have deserved it. Good luck on your journey.